PAULA PRYKE'S
wreaths & garlands

PAULA PRYKE'S
wreaths & garlands

Paula Pryke
photography by James Merrell

RYLAND
PETERS
& SMALL
LONDON NEW YORK

First published in Great Britain in 1998 and
reissued with amendments in 2004
by Ryland Peters & Small
Kirkman House
12–14 Whitfield Street
London W1T 2RP
www.rylandpeters.com

10 9 8 7 6 5 4 3 2 1

Printed in China

ISBN 1 84172 722 9

A CIP catalogue record for this book
is available from the British Library.

For this edition:
Designer Megan Smith
Editors Clare Double and Lesley Malkin
Production Paul Harding
Art Director Gabriella Le Grazie
Publishing Director Alison Starling

Illustrator Helen Smythe
Stylists   Martin Bourne
         Margaret Caselton
         Nato Welton

contents

introduction

Throughout the world, in every culture, circles, rings, wreaths, garlands and swags of fresh and dried plant materials have always been steeped in symbolism and meaning. The wreath, in particular, has come to signify eternal love, friendship, remembrance and even life itself. At both religious and secular events, these decorations have had a role to play – floral headdresses were worn by both bride and groom as a symbol of purity, and flower garlands were, and still are, offered as a greeting to guests in many countries.

Although the craft of wreath- and garland-making dates back to ancient Greece and Rome, it is still popular today, having never really disappeared from our collective experience. By weaving flowers into wreaths, we are continuing a long tradition of designing circular forms for healing or spiritual wellbeing as well as for their own aesthetic value.

Contemporary wreaths, garlands and swags are essentially flower arrangements without containers and are designed to be displayed on or around doors or walls, draped around parasols and table edges, or worn as headdresses by brides and bridesmaids. Whatever its intended location or use, the modern wreath most commonly maintains its traditional circular shape, but can also be in the form of a heart or novelty shape, and is often associated with remembrance and respect for the dead. Garlands of flowers and foliage, on the other hand, have happier associations. These long, flexible floral decorations are suspended

horizontally or vertically from architectural or garden features. Large-scale garlands of fresh flowers are curled around pillars, marquee poles, or staircase banisters for dramatic effect, or hung in dainty chains around a table edge. Swags are typically vertical hanging decorations but they tend to be shorter and more compact than garlands. Often swags are simply hand-tied bunches of flowers that rely on the plant stems for support rather than being attached to a rigid or flexible wreath base.

The true craft of wreath-making is taking whatever is plentiful and inexpensive in nature and fashioning it into an imaginative decoration. Take pleasure in collecting objects, such as pebbles and driftwood from the seashore and enjoy the fact that each new season brings fresh materials for wreath-making. Even before I worked professionally with flowers, I took great delight in making fresh and dried displays from mushrooms and moss and other plant matter that I gathered on woodland walks. I particularly relished the season of autumn, when I could create simple wreaths out of garden leaves. Even though these displays were not extravagant or beautifully constructed, there was a sense of achievement to be gained in making my own decorations for the home.

Although the following pages are full of inspirational ideas and projects, I hope you will look upon them as a starting point for your own designs. I came to floristry after a career in teaching history and never considered myself artistic. Now that I work with flowers every day, I am constantly amazed at how each individual brings his or her own feel and look to a display, even when starting with identical materials. I think the secret of success is having the confidence to express your style. It is also important to plan the display to suit its location. Whether fresh or dried, wreaths and garlands are among the most beautiful natural embellishments we can bring into our lives. They are timeless art forms that we can make for ourselves and our friends.

Paula Pryke

room decorations

Festoons of flowers, foliage, herbs and fruit were first brought into the home to celebrate the harvest and to dry and store seeds; they are one of the earliest forms of floral display. Later, swags of decorative fruit and flowers became popular architectural details in room interiors and were carved from stone or wood or moulded from plaster. Today, the use of fresh wreaths as room decorations has undergone a revival – they are used to stunning effect as door, wall and table ornaments.

ABOVE Freeze-dried roses and bunches of dried lavender and marjoram make for a long-lasting, scented display. The heart-shaped base is wired onto a pole and inserted into a dry floral foam-filled pot. LEFT A cornucopia-shaped basket is decorated with sun-dried seed heads and strands of snake grass. Crown imperials fill a plastic container of water set into the basket to make a special door decoration.

ABOVE AND RIGHT These attractive paper flowers and dried and dyed red maize were bought from Native Americans in Arizona, USA. I have glued these treasures to a wreath sprayed blue as a reminder of the use of colour in the Southwest.

OPPOSITE TOP LEFT Crab apples last well in displays. Here, they have been wired onto a dry floral foam ring, to offer a warm welcome at an autumnal gathering.

OPPOSITE TOP CENTRE Adapt an old wreath frame to create a living wreath of mind-your-own-business plants. To do this, remove the foam, drill drainage holes in the base and fill with compost and plants.

OPPOSITE TOP RIGHT Hydrangea flower heads turn burgundy red in autumn. Packed into a floral foam ring, they dry naturally to form a permanent display.

LEFT Twig wreath bases provide the foundation for many fresh floral displays. Here, small phials of water are wired to the base to keep the blue cornflowers and scabious alive. Trailing ivy hides the base and shells add interest.

BELOW To make a modern Shaker-style decoration, simply cut Styrofoam™ into three large star shapes and glue red mung beans onto each one. Hang the stars from lengths of ribbon on a wooden coat rail.

seashell and starfish wreath

This permanent wreath design introduces a nautical theme to bathroom decoration. Select a mixture of mother-of-pearl, scallop, oyster, clam and spiral shells in a variety of shapes and sizes, and juxtapose their intricate patterns and smooth finishes with spiky, textural starfish and coils of heavy-duty rope.

MATERIALS & EQUIPMENT
2 circular wire frames, 75 cm (30 in) diameter

9 m (10 yds) rope, 5 cm (2 in) diameter

4 pieces driftwood, approximately 40 cm (16 in) long

6 mother-of-pearl shells • 2 yellow clam shells

3 cream conch shells • 7 brown-and-white striped conch shells

9 pearl-white spiral cones • 7 long brown spiral cones

4 oyster shells • 1 brown-and-white spiky shell

5 large brown mussel-type shells • 5 large cream mussel-type shells

11 large starfish • 11 small starfish • 8 fan-shaped scallop shells • selection of small shells

reel wire • wire cutters • scrap paper • silver spray paint • hot glue gun and glue sticks

1 Place one circular wire frame on top of the other. Bind the two frames together with reel wire to make an extra-strong base to take the weight of the rope and shells. Lay the double frame on scrap paper, spray it with silver paint and leave it to dry.

2 Hold one end of the rope and start coiling it loosely over the wire frame in an anticlockwise direction; make sure that the rope encircles the frame at least four times.

3 Arrange the coils of rope on the frame and, when you are happy with their position, use reel wire to bind the rope to the frame.

4 Evenly space the four pieces of driftwood around the wreath and then glue them securely in place on the rope.

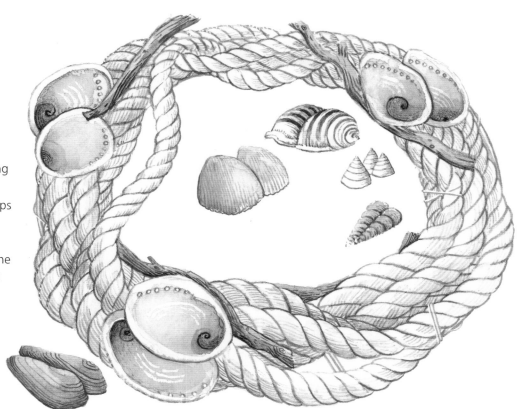

5 Decide which point is the top of the display, and then start gluing the larger shells onto the rope. Arrange the shells in pairs or groups of three, and try to balance the colours and shapes around the circular display. Work out where the starfish will have most impact and glue them into position.

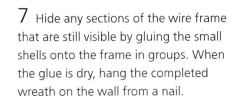

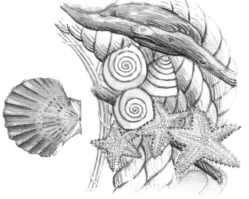

6 Save the scallop shells until last, and then use them to fill in any spaces between the wire frame and coils of rope.

7 Hide any sections of the wire frame that are still visible by gluing the small shells onto the frame in groups. When the glue is dry, hang the completed wreath on the wall from a nail.

everlasting heart
of roses

A delicate heart-shaped wreath covered in freeze-dried red roses and
sprigs of dried purple lavender makes an eye-catching wall display.
Freeze-drying is a specialist technique that preserves the natural beauty
of the rose petals; the dried roses do not become brittle and
disintegrate but look spectacular for months to come.

MATERIALS & EQUIPMENT

heart-shaped straw wreath, 45 cm (18 in) across at widest point

1 m (1 yd) deep purple rope, 1 cm (½ in) diameter

3 m (3¾ yds) red hessian ribbon, 8 cm (3 in) wide

25 bunches dried lavender (*Lavandula*), 5–8 stems per bunch

46 freeze-dried roses (*Rosa*)

30 glycerined galax leaves (*Galax*)

reel wire • wire cutters

glue • florist's scissors

medium-gauge stub wires

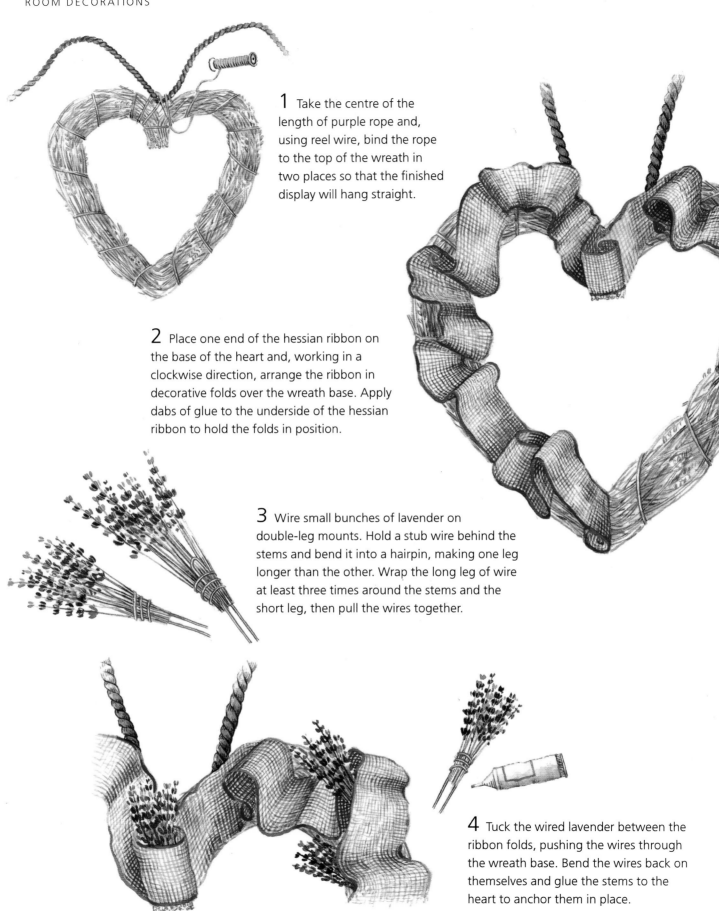

1 Take the centre of the length of purple rope and, using reel wire, bind the rope to the top of the wreath in two places so that the finished display will hang straight.

2 Place one end of the hessian ribbon on the base of the heart and, working in a clockwise direction, arrange the ribbon in decorative folds over the wreath base. Apply dabs of glue to the underside of the hessian ribbon to hold the folds in position.

3 Wire small bunches of lavender on double-leg mounts. Hold a stub wire behind the stems and bend it into a hairpin, making one leg longer than the other. Wrap the long leg of wire at least three times around the stems and the short leg, then pull the wires together.

4 Tuck the wired lavender between the ribbon folds, pushing the wires through the wreath base. Bend the wires back on themselves and glue the stems to the heart to anchor them in place.

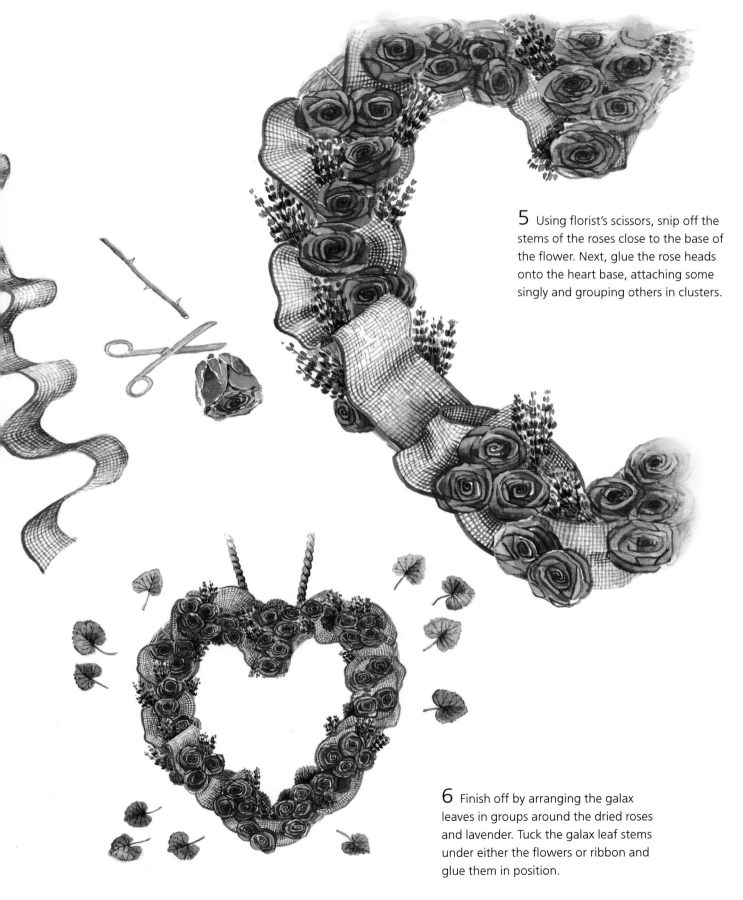

5 Using florist's scissors, snip off the stems of the roses close to the base of the flower. Next, glue the rose heads onto the heart base, attaching some singly and grouping others in clusters.

6 Finish off by arranging the galax leaves in groups around the dried roses and lavender. Tuck the galax leaf stems under either the flowers or ribbon and glue them in position.

horseshoe of succulents

The horseshoe is a symbol of good luck in many cultures. This attractive horseshoe wreath is created using a variety of succulent species. These popular house and garden plants are ideal subjects for living wreaths as, once their roots are embedded in a damp mossy base, they need only small amounts of water and nutrients to survive.

MATERIALS & EQUIPMENT

5-mm (¼-in) chicken wire, 120 x 30 cm (48 x 12 in)

damp sphagnum moss

plastic bin liner

30 mixed succulent plants (*Echeveria*)

reel wire • wire cutters • florist's scissors

german pins • medium-gauge stub wires

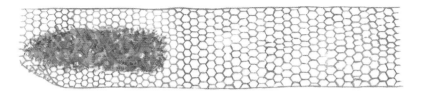

1 Lay the strip of chicken wire flat on the work surface and place a clump of damp sphagnum moss at one end.

2 Tease the moss along the centre of the chicken wire and, as you work, wrap the edges around the moss. Then, using reel wire, tightly bind the chicken wire to create a sausage shape. Add further clumps of moss, working your way along the length of the chicken wire, adding extra moss when you reach the centre to make it fatter there.

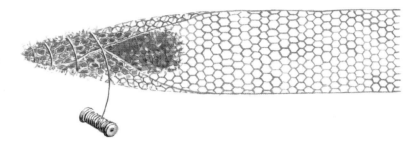

3 When you have completed the sausage shape, knot and cut the reel wire. Next, trim back any straggly pieces of moss so that the moss sits close to the frame.

4 Bend the two ends of the sausage shape together to make a horseshoe. Then, turn the frame over and line the back with plastic to prevent the damp moss from damaging the wall. To do this, cut up a plastic bin liner into several 10 cm (4 in) strips. Fasten a strip of plastic to the top edge of the horseshoe with a german pin. Fold the plastic in a zigzag, pinning as you go, so that it follows the edge of the frame. Work your way around the back of the horseshoe until it is completely covered in plastic.

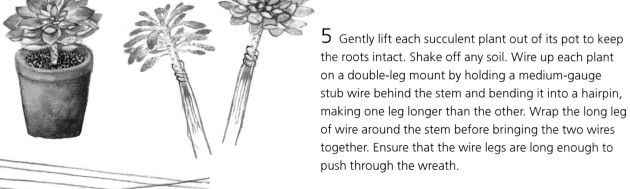

5 Gently lift each succulent plant out of its pot to keep the roots intact. Shake off any soil. Wire up each plant on a double-leg mount by holding a medium-gauge stub wire behind the stem and bending it into a hairpin, making one leg longer than the other. Wrap the long leg of wire around the stem before bringing the two wires together. Ensure that the wire legs are long enough to push through the wreath.

6 Begin by attaching the larger succulents to the horseshoe. To attach the plants, hold the stub wires at a 45° angle to the base and push them through the moss. Bend the wires back on themselves to anchor the plant.

7 Keep wiring the larger succulent plants to the horseshoe as described in step 6. Space the plants evenly around the frame to balance the display.

8 Continue wiring plants to the frame, using the technique shown in step 6. Try to balance the colours, sizes and textures of the different succulents. Lastly, fill in any gaps on the horseshoe with smaller plants. Spray-mist the display with water every two weeks to keep the moss base moist. This way, the rooted succulents will have a longer life.

gardening-theme wreath

For the gardening enthusiast, a wreath decorated with seed packets, scarecrow dolls, miniature gnomes, flowerpots, watering cans and other novelty items, makes an original and personal gift. Hung on the potting shed or kitchen door, it will be a constant source of delight throughout the gardening year.

MATERIALS & EQUIPMENT

circular twig wreath, 50 cm (20 in) diameter

honeysuckle vine (*Lonicera*), approximately 3 m (10 ft)

dried carpet moss

5 novelty watering cans

5 terracotta flowerpots, 5–9 cm (2–3½ in) high

2 decorative fences, 10 cm (4 in) high, 20 cm (8 in) long

4 pieces driftwood, 15–20 cm (6–8 in) long

garden trowel and fork

3 m (3¼ yds) beige hessian ribbon, 5 cm (2 in) wide

10 dried mushrooms • 5 packets of seeds

3 garden gnomes, 9 cm (3½ in) tall • 4 scarecrow dolls, 9 cm (3½ in) tall

reel wire • wire cutters • medium-gauge stub wires • glue

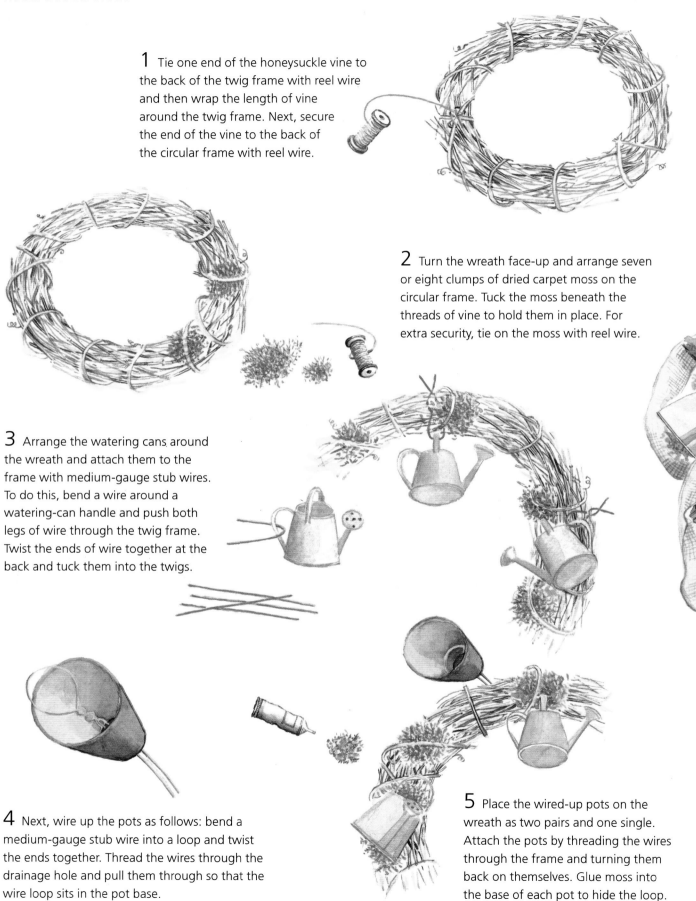

1 Tie one end of the honeysuckle vine to the back of the twig frame with reel wire and then wrap the length of vine around the twig frame. Next, secure the end of the vine to the back of the circular frame with reel wire.

2 Turn the wreath face-up and arrange seven or eight clumps of dried carpet moss on the circular frame. Tuck the moss beneath the threads of vine to hold them in place. For extra security, tie on the moss with reel wire.

3 Arrange the watering cans around the wreath and attach them to the frame with medium-gauge stub wires. To do this, bend a wire around a watering-can handle and push both legs of wire through the twig frame. Twist the ends of wire together at the back and tuck them into the twigs.

4 Next, wire up the pots as follows: bend a medium-gauge stub wire into a loop and twist the ends together. Thread the wires through the drainage hole and pull them through so that the wire loop sits in the pot base.

5 Place the wired-up pots on the wreath as two pairs and one single. Attach the pots by threading the wires through the frame and turning them back on themselves. Glue moss into the base of each pot to hide the loop.

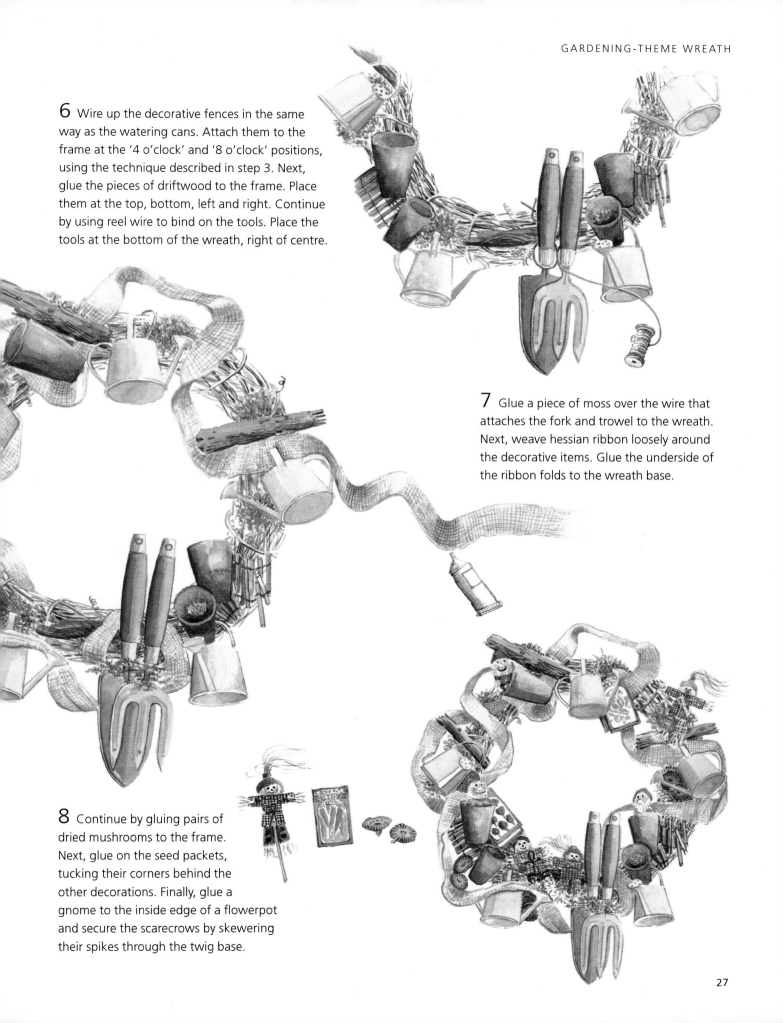

6 Wire up the decorative fences in the same way as the watering cans. Attach them to the frame at the '4 o'clock' and '8 o'clock' positions, using the technique described in step 3. Next, glue the pieces of driftwood to the frame. Place them at the top, bottom, left and right. Continue by using reel wire to bind on the tools. Place the tools at the bottom of the wreath, right of centre.

7 Glue a piece of moss over the wire that attaches the fork and trowel to the wreath. Next, weave hessian ribbon loosely around the decorative items. Glue the underside of the ribbon folds to the wreath base.

8 Continue by gluing pairs of dried mushrooms to the frame. Next, glue on the seed packets, tucking their corners behind the other decorations. Finally, glue a gnome to the inside edge of a flowerpot and secure the scarecrows by skewering their spikes through the twig base.

driftwood frame

Wood gnarled and bleached by the sun adds a primitive beauty to any
room interior, and here a rectangular wire frame offers a rigid base on
which to show off these driftwood treasures. The beauty of this arrangement
is that it is simple and inexpensive to produce and works well as a unique
and eye-catching detail against any backdrop. Half the fun of this
creation is collecting the material from a park or seashore and piecing
together this woody jigsaw puzzle.

MATERIALS & EQUIPMENT

rectangular wire frame, 60 x 45 cm (24 x 18 in)

8 large pieces of driftwood

40 driftwood twigs

1 large, flat pebble

fine-grade sandpaper

reel wire • wire cutters

natural string • scissors

hot glue gun and glue sticks

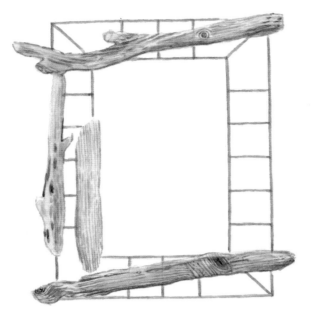

1 Lay out your pieces of driftwood and the rectangular wire frame on a flat, non-scratch surface. Work out the best way to arrange the wood on the frame; the largest piece will probably look best along the bottom edge. Using fine-grade sandpaper, smooth away any protrusions on the underside of the wood pieces so that they will lie flush with the frame.

2 Using reel wire, bind each piece of wood securely onto the wire frame and then cut the wire with wire cutters. Fasten the longer pieces of wood at both ends, to hold them in position on the frame.

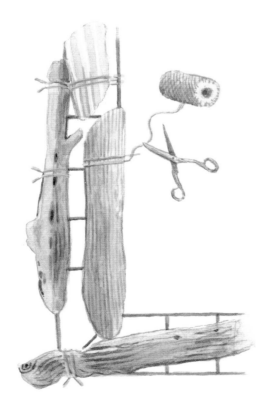

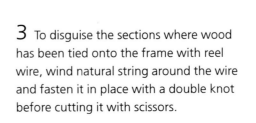

3 To disguise the sections where wood has been tied onto the frame with reel wire, wind natural string around the wire and fasten it in place with a double knot before cutting it with scissors.

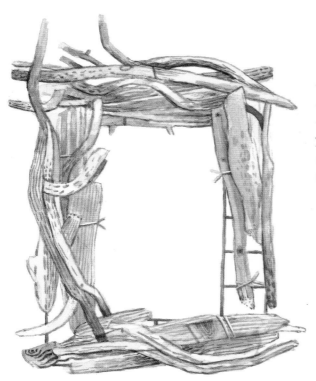

4 Build up the driftwood frame by arranging smaller pieces of wood on top of the main structure. When you are happy that these smaller pieces fill in the gaps, glue them in place on the frame.

5 Finish off the frame by gluing on small twigs. Use them to fill in any gaps between the larger pieces of wood and also to hide areas where the wire frame is still visible.

6 Finally, glue the large pebble onto the bottom left-hand corner of the frame. When the glue is dry, hang the frame on a nail, or tie a loop of reel wire to the frame and hang it from a strong picture hook.

silk-covered button ring

Put your sewing skills to the test by creating this striking purple silk ring, studded with an assortment of buttons. Inspired by London's fruit and vegetable sellers, known as the pearly kings and queens, who were famous for decorating their clothes with a lavish collection of pearl buttons, this wreath is both rich and textural.

MATERIALS & EQUIPMENT

circular twig wreath, 55 cm (22 in) diameter

2 x 225 g (8 oz) polyester wadding strips,
175 x 35 cm (70 x 14 in), joined end-to-end

purple raw silk, 175 x 37.5 cm (70 x 15 in)

200 buttons in a selection of colours, shapes and sizes

1 m (1 yd) red rope, 1 cm (½ in) diameter

scissors • needle • haberdashery pins

purple thread plus an assortment of other colours

1 Wrap the strip of polyester wadding tightly around the twig wreath, like a bandage, to form a padded base. Ensure that the edges of the fabric overlap one another so that none of the wreath is visible.

2 When the wreath is covered, trim the end of the fabric and tack it in place with a row of neat stitches.

3 Hem the two ends of the strip of silk together. Then lay the silk in a circle on your work surface, right-side down. Place the 'bandaged' wreath on top. Adjust the silk so the ring sits in the centre, arranging the inner edge in even folds until you are happy with the way the silk fits.

4 Bring a section of the purple silk around the padded ring. Fold both raw edges of the silk under, tuck the outer edge underneath the inner edge and then pin them in place.

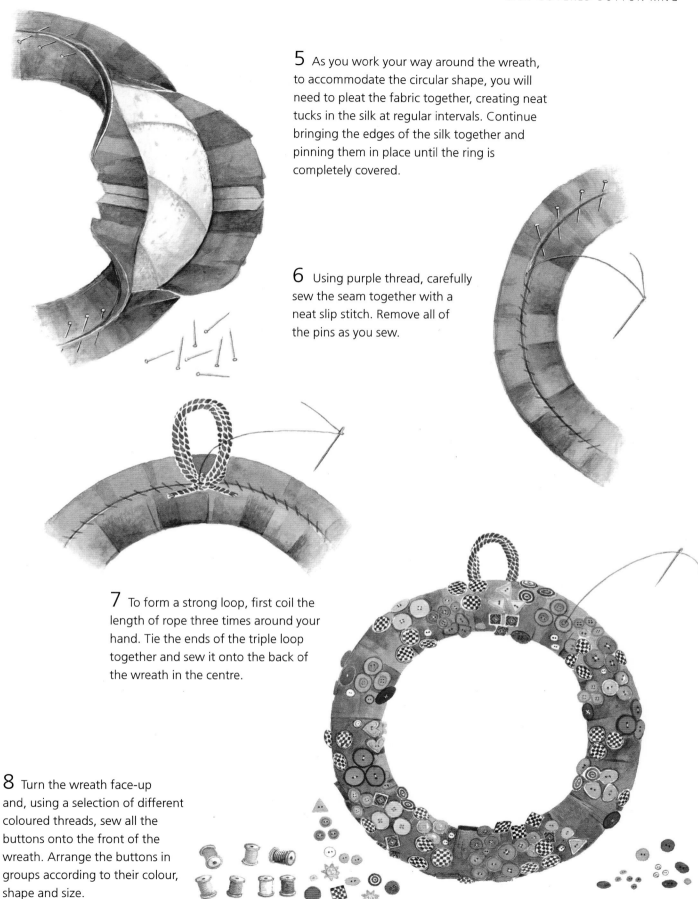

5 As you work your way around the wreath, to accommodate the circular shape, you will need to pleat the fabric together, creating neat tucks in the silk at regular intervals. Continue bringing the edges of the silk together and pinning them in place until the ring is completely covered.

6 Using purple thread, carefully sew the seam together with a neat slip stitch. Remove all of the pins as you sew.

7 To form a strong loop, first coil the length of rope three times around your hand. Tie the ends of the triple loop together and sew it onto the back of the wreath in the centre.

8 Turn the wreath face-up and, using a selection of different coloured threads, sew all the buttons onto the front of the wreath. Arrange the buttons in groups according to their colour, shape and size.

ABOVE This traditional kissing ball is made by wiring sprigs of mistletoe into damp sphagnum moss in two hanging baskets. **LEFT** Corn is an important symbol in Thanksgiving celebrations and, here, dried cobs of corn are tied with brightly coloured raffia to a circular twig frame.

seasonal wreaths

For thousands of years, the variety and abundance of flowers, fruits and foliage available at different times of the year have been used to mark the great seasonal events. During the winter months, pine and mistletoe are abundant and consequently form the backbone of Christmas displays, while golden corn and wreaths of leaves celebrate autumn festivals. In spring and summer, the wealth of fresh flowers available produces stunning floral displays.

OPPOSITE TOP Shimmering silver and purple ribbon, as well as orange fruits and spices decorate this blue pine wreath.
TOP OF PAGE Preserved magnolia leaves maintain their glossy dark green sheen and distinctive shape and look stunning on their own in a classic-style wreath.

CENTRE LEFT A snowflake frame of blue pine is simple to make; just wire six garden canes together with reel wire at the centre point, and add the foliage.
BOTTOM LEFT To make a living wreath, bind potted plants to a frame. These miniature roses take pride of place on a garden wall.

ABOVE Mixed coloured ranunculi, with their dark centres, are one of my favourite flowers because of their cheerful faces. Bind the stems with rope and pack them in a jar of water covered by sacking. Tie them to the gate to show where the party is being held.

candle centrepiece

Candlelight adds to the special atmosphere when you entertain outdoors. Here, a mosaic-style storm lamp is encircled by a rich mix of indigo delphiniums and purple bluebells and anemones, offset by white ranunculi and starflowers, and green guelder rose and ivy, to make a striking centrepiece. By covering the candle in a storm lamp, you can keep the flame alive in a breeze and prevent molten wax from dripping over the flowers and table.

MATERIALS & EQUIPMENT

glass mosaic storm lamp and nightlight candle

circular floral foam base, 36 cm (15 in) diameter

6 stems fruiting ivy (*Hedera*), 2 groups of 3

9 sprigs guelder rose (*Viburnum opulus*), 3 groups of 3

14 purple anemones (*Anemone coronaria*), 2 groups of 7

8 white ranunculi (*Ranunculus*)

10 blue delphiniums (*Delphinium* 'Blue Bees'), 2 groups of 5

10 starflowers (*Ornithogalum montanum*), 2 groups of 5

10 bluebells (*Scilla*)

florist's knife • florist's scissors

1 Soak the foam base in water for five minutes. Then, using a florist's knife, shave off about 2.5 cm (1 in) from both the inner and outer top edge of the foam in order to give the ring a bevelled profile.

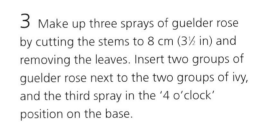

2 Cut six stems of fruiting ivy, 8 cm (3½ in) long. Make two small sprays of three stems each, and then insert the two groups into the circular foam base at '12 o'clock' and '9 o'clock' positions.

3 Make up three sprays of guelder rose by cutting the stems to 8 cm (3½ in) and removing the leaves. Insert two groups of guelder rose next to the two groups of ivy, and the third spray in the '4 o'clock' position on the base.

4 Next, add the larger flowers. Cut the stems of the anemones and ranunculi to 5 cm (2 in). Divide the anemones into two groups of seven flowers and, working from the outer to the inner edge of the ring, place them at '2 o'clock' and '6 o'clock'. Insert the ranunculi as one group at the '10 o'clock' position.

5 Continue with the delicate starflowers, delphiniums and bluebells. Cut all the stems to 8 cm (3½ in) long, and remove the leaves. Divide the starflowers and delphiniums into two groups. Place each group of starflowers next to the groups of anemones on the ring. Add the delphiniums at the '5 o'clock' and '11 o'clock' positions. Insert the bluebells in a single group into the '7 o'clock' position on the circular floral foam base.

6 Make sure that the entire base is filled in with fresh flowers and foliage and then place the display in situ. Put the candle-holder base and nightlight candle in the centre of the flower ring. Light the candle with a taper and cover with the hood of the storm lamp.

sunflower garland

For a special summer party, decorate a garden parasol with swags of vivid yellow sunflowers and yarrow, red chilli peppers and soft green scented herbs, bound onto a length of garden string. While this garland is simple to make, the choice of plant material is important because the flowers and foliage must be able to survive out of water without drooping. For a longer-lasting garland, attach the flowers and foliage to a pre-soaked floral foam base.

MATERIALS & EQUIPMENT

for a parasol with a 2.5 m (8 ft) diameter, you will need to make a garland
8 m (26 ft) long; make it in eight separate 1 m (1 yd) sections.

for 1 m (1 yd) of garland:

10 sunflowers (*Helianthus*)

12 sprigs fruiting ivy (*Hedera*)

17 clusters fresh red ornamental chilli peppers (*Capsicum*)

10 stems dill (*Anethum graveolens*)

7 yellow yarrow (*Achillea* 'Moonshine')

12 leucospermum (*Leucospermum cordifolium*)

garden string • florist's scissors • reel wire • wire cutters • needle and thread

1 Work out how much string you need by taking it around the bottom edge of the parasol. Leave enough slack in the string to create a generous swag of flowers and foliage between each spoke. Allow a further 30 cm (12 in) at each end of the string to tie the garland to the parasol.

2 Soak the flowers in water for up to 12 hours. Cut the stems of the flowers and foliage to 20 cm (8 in) in length. Strip off the lower leaves from the stems and, on a work surface, organize the plant matter into groups according to type.

3 Start binding flowers and foliage onto the string, 30 cm (12 in) from one end. Lay a sunflower stem against the string and bind it on tightly with reel wire. Next, place a bunch of fruiting ivy on top of the sunflower stem, close to the flower head, and bind this on with reel wire. Follow the ivy with two or three stems of chillies and a leucospermum. As you work, cut off the stem ends to make it easier for you to attach the next group.

4 Continue by wiring on sprays of dill to soften the effect. Follow this with a single yellow yarrow, a cluster of chilli peppers and sprigs of fruiting ivy. Keep turning the string as you work so that the material is bound on in a spiral manner to create an all-round display.

5 At this stage, bind in the next sunflower. These large flower heads, like the yellow yarrow, are bold enough to stand on their own in the display and do not need to be added in groups like the more delicate plant material.

6 Follow the single sunflower with sprigs of dill, chilli peppers, a single leucospermum, another sunflower and yellow yarrow. Keep making sure that the flowers and foliage are packed together and are arranged in a spiral so that the string is covered.

7 Continue with the following sequence: sprays of dill; chilli peppers; fruiting ivy; leucospermum; sunflower; fruiting ivy; chilli peppers; yellow yarrow; sunflower. Start the sequence again from step 3 and continue binding on material until you are 30 cm (12 in) from the end of the string.

8 The finished garland will be very heavy so attach it to the spokes of the parasol section by section, using lengths of string. If necessary, you can also stitch the garland to the parasol fabric halfway between each spoke. Spray-mist the garland with water to keep it fresh.

ring of autumn leaves

Rich red and orange beech leaves, preserved in glycerine, are used to construct a glowing autumnal display. This method of drying plant material captures seasonal colours and prevents dried leaves from becoming dull and brittle. Available from specialist florists, glycerined leaves look stunning for six months or more.

MATERIALS & EQUIPMENT

for a wreath 50 cm (20 in) in diameter:

30 lengths honeysuckle vine (*Lonicera*), 1.6 m (5 ft)

20 branches glycerined beech leaves (*Fagus*)

florist's scissors • reel wire • wire cutters

medium-gauge stub wires • heavy-gauge stub wire

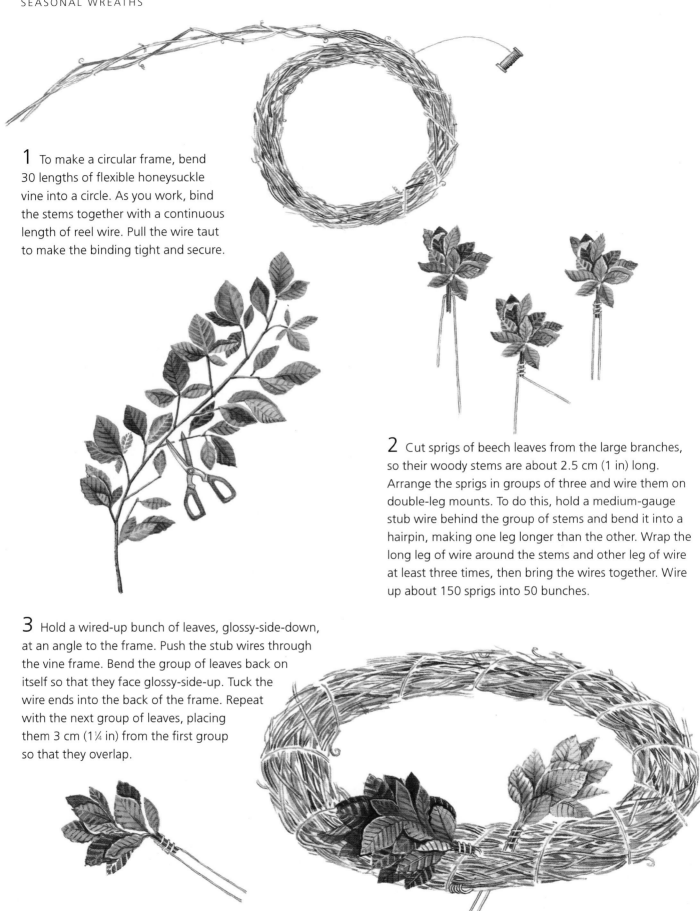

1 To make a circular frame, bend
30 lengths of flexible honeysuckle
vine into a circle. As you work, bind
the stems together with a continuous
length of reel wire. Pull the wire taut
to make the binding tight and secure.

2 Cut sprigs of beech leaves from the large branches,
so their woody stems are about 2.5 cm (1 in) long.
Arrange the sprigs in groups of three and wire them on
double-leg mounts. To do this, hold a medium-gauge
stub wire behind the group of stems and bend it into a
hairpin, making one leg longer than the other. Wrap the
long leg of wire around the stems and other leg of wire
at least three times, then bring the wires together. Wire
up about 150 sprigs into 50 bunches.

3 Hold a wired-up bunch of leaves, glossy-side-down,
at an angle to the frame. Push the stub wires through
the vine frame. Bend the group of leaves back on
itself so that they face glossy-side-up. Tuck the
wire ends into the back of the frame. Repeat
with the next group of leaves, placing
them 3 cm (1¼ in) from the first group
so that they overlap.

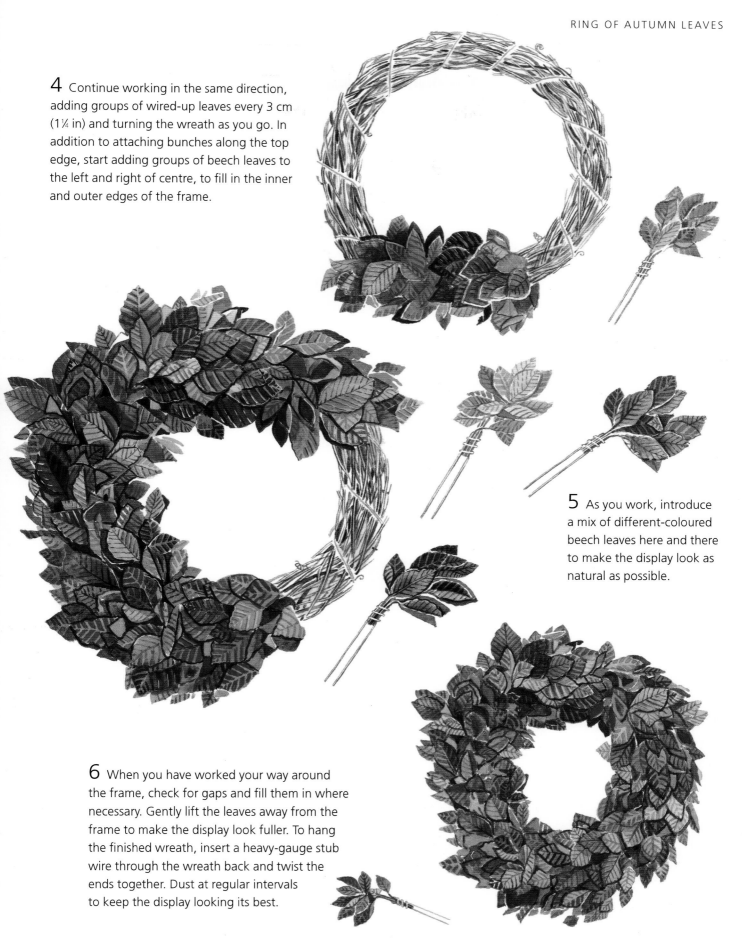

4 Continue working in the same direction, adding groups of wired-up leaves every 3 cm (1¼ in) and turning the wreath as you go. In addition to attaching bunches along the top edge, start adding groups of beech leaves to the left and right of centre, to fill in the inner and outer edges of the frame.

5 As you work, introduce a mix of different-coloured beech leaves here and there to make the display look as natural as possible.

6 When you have worked your way around the frame, check for gaps and fill them in where necessary. Gently lift the leaves away from the frame to make the display look fuller. To hang the finished wreath, insert a heavy-gauge stub wire through the wreath back and twist the ends together. Dust at regular intervals to keep the display looking its best.

christmas wreath

Extend a warm welcome to guests during the festive season by decorating
the front door with a Christmas wreath. The custom of bringing greenery into
the home dates back to pagan times, when evergreen foliage was brought
inside for the winter solstice. Here, soft branches of blue pine entwined with
shimmering gold ribbon, small cones and clusters of cinnamon sticks and dried
orange slices release a heady mix of spicy and pine-scented aromas.

MATERIALS & EQUIPMENT

circular wire frame, 42.5 cm (17 in) diameter

sphagnum moss

plastic bin liner

5 branches blue pine (*Abies nobilis*)

gold cherub

6 dried orange slices

6 pine cones

24 cinnamon sticks, 6 groups of 4

60 cm (24 in) blue ribbon, 1.5 cm (⅝ in) wide

2.5 m (2¾ yds) gold ribbon, 5 cm (2 in) wide

reel wire • wire cutters • florist's scissors • german pins

medium-gauge stub wires • heavy-gauge stub wires

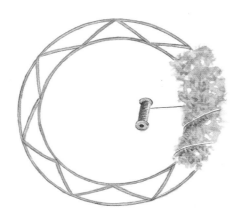

1 Dampen the sphagnum moss and remove any leaves and bark. Take a large clump of moss and tease it out over the wire frame. Secure the moss in place by binding it with reel wire. Continue adding moss and wiring it to the frame until the circle is covered.

2 To prevent the damp moss from leaking, line the back of the frame with plastic. Cut a plastic bin liner into 10 cm (4 in) strips. Fasten a strip of plastic to the edge of the wreath with a german pin. Fold the plastic in a zigzag, pinning as you go, so that it follows the frame. Cover the whole back in this way.

3 Cut the pine into lengths of 15 cm (6 in) and 10 cm (4 in). Using two medium-gauge stub wires, pin a long piece of pine to the outer edge of the frame. To do this, bend the stub wires into U-shapes and straddle a pine stem in two places with the wires. Push the wires through the moss base and bend them back on themselves to anchor them.

4 Using the same technique as described in step 3, pin a 10-cm (4-in) length of blue pine to the inner edge. Continue working your way around the wire base, overlapping branches of pine on the inner and outer edge until the whole wreath is covered.

5 Next, wire up the wreath decorations. Hook a heavy-gauge stub wire around the cherub's wings and twist the ends of the wire together. Next, wire up two groups of three orange slices. Thread a medium-gauge stub wire through the fruit flesh, bend it into a hairpin and twist the wires together. To wire a cone, slide a heavy-gauge stub wire around the scales of the cone and, again, twist the wires together. Arrange the cinnamon sticks into six groups. Bind each group with a 10 cm (4 in) length of blue ribbon. Thread a heavy-gauge stub wire through the ribbon knot and twist the wires together.

6 Secure the cherub at the top of the wreath by pushing the wires through the moss base. Insert the orange slices above and below the cherub's left wing, again pushing the wires through the moss. Place three groups of cinnamon at '3 o'clock' and three at '9 o'clock'. Next, place the cones in two groups of three at '1 o'clock' and '8 o'clock'. Cut 1.5 m (1⅝ yds) of the gold ribbon and weave it around the wreath.

7 To make the bow, cut two pieces of gold ribbon, each 50 cm (20 in) long. Fold one length into two loops and pinch the loops together in the centre. Take the second ribbon and tie it in a single knot around the loops.

8 To finish, hook a medium-gauge stub wire through the bow and secure it to the bottom of the wreath by pushing the stub wires through the moss base and bending them back on themselves.

LEFT Roses and sprigs of skimmia make a perfect scented hanging ball for a special party or wedding. To make the ball, cut a block of wet floral foam to shape. Tie a cord around the centre of the foam and insert the skimmia and roses. Handle the roses carefully to avoid bruising the petals. BELOW Sweet-scented stephanotis has been wound around a circle to produce a simple, dainty bridesmaid's ring. BOTTOM OF PAGE A mix of fragrant herbs and flowers are wired onto a small bridesmaid's basket, which is filled with sweets to offer to guests. OPPOSITE, TOP OF PAGE Richly scented blue hyacinth bulbs are planted in a wire frame that has been filled with compost and covered with carpet moss to hold moisture within the wreath.

scented wreaths

Bringing leaves, flowers, roots and bark into the home to fill each room with fragrance has always been popular; the original scented wreath for the home may have been a circle of bay leaves, sacred to the Greek god Apollo. Choose flowers and foliage to grow in the garden for their fragrance as well as their appearance and carefully select the plant materials you bring indoors. Silver foliage plants, such as blue pine or eucalyptus with their fresh woody scent, work well, as do richly fragrant flowers, such as hyacinths, stephanotis, roses and lilies, whose heady scents will linger in the room.

ABOVE A star-shaped wire frame has been covered with moss and sprigs of fragrant blue pine to create a welcoming Christmas wreath.

LEFT Silver-grey eucalyptus pods are bound onto a circular frame using reel wire. The fragrance of the buds can be very strong, so the wreath is best hung outside so as not to be overpowering.

heart of fresh roses

A heart-shaped foam base, available ready-made from floral foam
manufacturers, is the perfect frame for a delicate display of fragrant pale
pink 'Anna' roses, palest green guelder rose and lacy white hydrangeas.
Suspend the heart from a length of green velvet ribbon for the finishing
touch to this romantic token for a summer wedding or engagement party.

MATERIALS & EQUIPMENT

heart-shaped floral foam base, 43 cm (17 in) across at widest point

50 cm (20 in) green velvet ribbon, 3.5 cm (1½ in) wide

30 pink roses (*Rosa* 'Anna')

27 sprigs guelder rose (*Viburnum opulus*)

6 white hydrangeas (*Hydrangea macrophylla*)

florist's knife • heavy-gauge stub wire • florist's scissors

1 Soak the heart-shaped foam base in water for five minutes. Then, using a florist's knife, trim away a strip of foam about 2.5 cm (1 in) wide on both the inner and outer edges; this will make the base more three-dimensional.

2 Tie the velvet ribbon with which to hang the display around the top of the heart base and fasten it in place with a double knot. To stop the ribbon from slipping, bend a heavy-gauge stub wire into a U-shape and insert it into the foam; straddling the ribbon, pinning it in place.

3 Using florist's scissors, trim the stems of the roses to within 5 cm (2 in) of the rose heads. Arrange the roses around the heart shape, inserting the stems so that the flowers face to the right and left of the base.

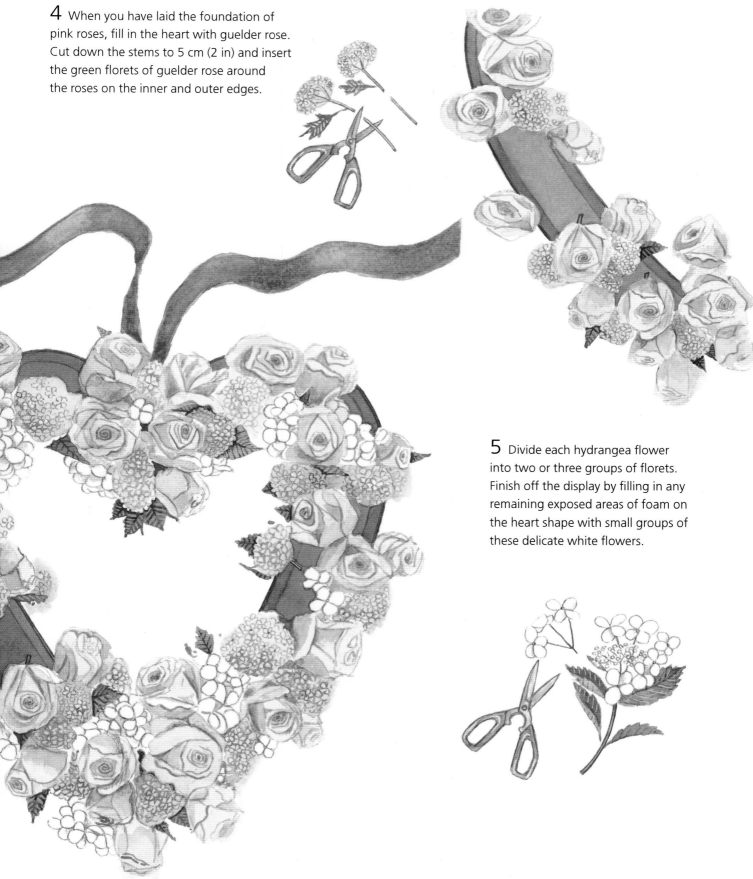

4 When you have laid the foundation of pink roses, fill in the heart with guelder rose. Cut down the stems to 5 cm (2 in) and insert the green florets of guelder rose around the roses on the inner and outer edges.

5 Divide each hydrangea flower into two or three groups of florets. Finish off the display by filling in any remaining exposed areas of foam on the heart shape with small groups of these delicate white flowers.

personalized gardenia display

White gardenias are one of the most exquisite of scented plants and are popular with brides the world over. Their creamy flowers and waxy foliage make elegant displays with a wonderful perfume. A personalized decoration such as this, in the shape of an initial or number, would be perfect for a birthday, wedding or anniversary.

MATERIALS & EQUIPMENT

floral foam designer board, 30 x 50 cm (12 x 20 in)

square pot, 20 x 20 cm (8 x 8 in), 25 cm (10 in) high

wooden pole, 50 cm (20 in) long • 4 handfuls gravel

2 stems clematis vine (*Clematis vitalba*), approximately 1 m (3 ft)

gold spray paint • scrap paper

4 medium-sized gardenia plants (*Gardenia*)

pencil and paper • florist's knife

medium-gauge stub wires • pebbles

florist's tape • wire cutters • florist's scissors

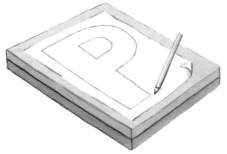

1 Draw a paper template for your letter about 40 cm (16 in) tall and 25 cm (10 in) wide, at the widest point. This scale will ensure that the letter board is strong and thick enough to carry the gardenia flowers.

2 With a florist's knife, score around the edge of the letter – here a P – to transfer the design to the board. Cut out the shape using the scored line as a guide.

3 Place the square pot, the gravel, the pole, the P-shaped board (face-down), the clematis vine and some clematis twigs on scrap paper. Spray the items gold (on all sides, except for the P) and allow to dry.

4 Soak the P-shape in water for ten minutes, then push about 25 cm (10 in) of the pole into the letter base. If necessary, bind the pole and designer board together with florist's tape to make it secure.

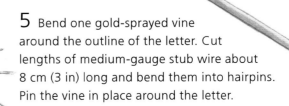

5 Bend one gold-sprayed vine around the outline of the letter. Cut lengths of medium-gauge stub wire about 8 cm (3 in) long and bend them into hairpins. Pin the vine in place around the letter.

6 Cut sprigs of flowers and foliage about 5 cm (2 in) long, but reserve the flowering stems for the top surface of the P-shape. Insert the leaf stems into the board around the sides of the P-shape. Use even shorter leaf stems for the inner edge of the central hole.

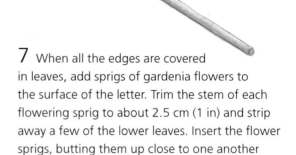

7 When all the edges are covered in leaves, add sprigs of gardenia flowers to the surface of the letter. Trim the stem of each flowering sprig to about 2.5 cm (1 in) and strip away a few of the lower leaves. Insert the flower sprigs, butting them up close to one another around the board.

8 To visually soften the P-shaped outline, add a handful of gold twigs to the edge of the display. Make sure that the twigs face in different directions so they look natural.

9 Lastly, part-fill the pot with large pebbles to weigh it down. Insert the letter on its pole and, when it is straight, add the rest of the stones. Sprinkle a layer of gold gravel on top. To finish, twist a length of gold-sprayed clematis vine around the pole and display the finished letter face out.

wreath of lilies and apples

I enjoy using fruit and flowers together and, here, crisp green apples and
beautiful scented white lilies offer a fresh lime-green mix of plant material.
The white lilies sit on pre-soaked floral foam blocks but, even so, be warned
the display will have a limited life because the wired-up apples release
a natural gas that ages plant materials.

MATERIALS & EQUIPMENT

circular honeysuckle vine wreath, 55 cm (22 in) diameter

carpet moss

3 small caged dome-shaped blocks of floral foam with screw-in bases (Le Bump™)

18 green apples

9 sprigs fruiting ivy (*Hedera*)

3 white hydrangeas (*Hydrangea*)

2 pure white lilies (*Lilium* 'Casa Blanca')

6 white lilies with creamy yellow centres (*Lilium* 'Pompeii')

3 lengths trailing ivy (*Hedera*), 20–30 cm (8–12 in)

medium-gauge stub wires • florist's scissors

1 Divide the damp carpet moss into three clumps, approximately 10 cm (4 in) long. Arrange the clumps an equal distance apart, at three points on the wreath. This flat, damp moss does not need to be glued in place; simply tuck the corners of each clump under the vine binding on the wreath base.

2 Next, soak the three floral foam domes in water for five minutes. Position each one on the wreath between the moss, and screw their coiled bases through the open-weave base. To hold the domes in place, thread medium-gauge stub wires through the floral foam on both sides. Bend each wire into a hairpin and push the ends through the wreath and back on themselves.

3 To wire up the apples, push a length of medium-gauge stub wire through the bottom third of each fruit. Twist one leg of wire around the other and bring them together. Place three apples on each clump of moss and three around each dome. Push the stub wires through the wreath base and bind them around the vine at the back of the wreath.

4 To keep the flowers and foliage alive for as long as possible, arrange them on the pre-soaked floral foam domes. Begin with the fruiting ivy foliage. Trim the sprays to a length of 5 cm (2 in) and remove the lower leaves. Insert two or three sprigs of fruiting ivy into each dome.

5 Continue by adding the hydrangea heads. Trim their woody stems to 2.5 cm (1 in) and strip them of leaves. Insert one hydrangea into each of the three domes. Place the flowers on the lower edges of the foam and for added interest place one on the inner edge of the wreath and two on the outer edge.

6 Continue by trimming down the eight lily stems to 2.5 cm (1 in) and stripping the stems of any leaves. Insert the two 'Casa Blanca' lilies into one of the floral foam domes and insert three 'Pompeii' lilies into each of the other two domes.

7 Lastly, weave two or three lengths of trailing ivy, 20–30 cm (8–12 in) long, between the fresh flowers and foliage, to soften the overall effect. Insert the end of each ivy strand into a dome to keep it alive. Hang the finished display from a nail head. Spray-mist the moss and floral foam domes daily to keep them moist.

OPPOSITE TOP Small apples are wired to a moss frame by threading a stub wire through the apple flesh and twisting the ends together. Leaves and skimmia flowers help conceal the moss.

OPPOSITE BELOW LEFT Red ornamental chilli peppers are wired onto a single-wire wreath frame. Arrange the stalks end-to-end for variety and pack them tightly to conceal the wire base.

OPPOSITE BELOW RIGHT Store garlic in the kitchen by attaching raffia to the stalk of each garlic bulb and threading the bulbs onto a twig frame. Garlic cloves can be cut off as required for use in cooking.

LEFT Flowers and foliage can be used to decorate baskets of food for a party. Here, ivy and poppies are threaded through a twig basket which is filled with dried fruit and nuts. Wash all foliage very carefully when using it to decorate food.

ABOVE Children of all ages will love this, although they may not leave it alone. Cover a star-shaped wire frame with 1-cm (½-in) chicken wire, tie it onto a pole, and cement it into a pot. Spray the star gold and then leave it to dry while you tie ribbons onto all the sweet wrappers. Then attach the sweets to the wire to cover the star. Hide the cement with sweets, too.

ABOVE Terracotta pots filled with herbs and tied together with rope make a decorative roof-top or terrace display for the urban gardener.

RIGHT For a pretty summery look, make and hang a garland of flowers around a table. Choose a strong-headed flower, like marguerite daisies and thread the back of each flower head onto reel wire.

culinary themes

Foods, particularly breads, have long been associated with wreaths. The Egyptians fashioned bread into rings as a form of payment before the introduction of money, while in Greece, the family makes a circular wedding bread to symbolize wellbeing and good fortune. Above all, culinary wreaths are a useful and attractive way to store ingredients, such as chilli peppers, garlic and sweets, while food baskets and dessert tables look wonderful draped in flowers and foliage.

citrus-fruit ring

Groups of wired-up fresh oranges, lemons and limes surrounded by sprigs
of dark evergreen fruiting ivy leaves and berries make a striking winter wreath
of natural ingredients. The fruit adds texture, colour and scent to the display
at a time of year when flowers and foliage are in short supply. Place this
brightly coloured centrepiece on your dining room or kitchen table as
an imaginative alternative to a traditional bowl of winter fruits.

MATERIALS & EQUIPMENT

circular metal frame, 40 cm (16 in) diameter

sphagnum moss

80 bunches fruiting ivy (*Hedera*)

15 lemons • 15 oranges • 15 limes

reel wire • wire cutters

plastic bin liner • german pins

medium-gauge stub wires

florist's scissors

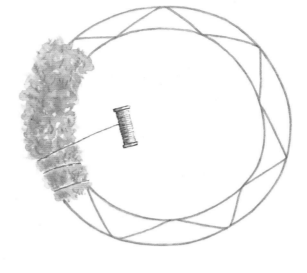

1 Dampen the sphagnum moss and tease it out to remove any loose leaves or bark. Take a large clump of moss and spread it along the frame. Secure the moss in place by binding it with reel wire. Continue adding moss and wiring it tightly to the frame until the circle is covered.

2 To prevent the damp moss wreath from leaking, line the back of the frame with plastic. To do this, cut a plastic bin liner into 10 cm (4 in) strips. Fasten a strip of plastic to the edge of the wreath with a german pin. Fold the plastic in a zigzag, pinning as you go, so that it follows the frame. Cover the whole frame circle in this way.

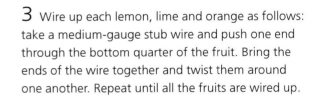

3 Wire up each lemon, lime and orange as follows: take a medium-gauge stub wire and push one end through the bottom quarter of the fruit. Bring the ends of the wire together and twist them around one another. Repeat until all the fruits are wired up.

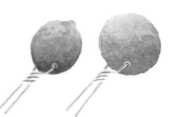

4 Begin by attaching the lemons to the wreath. Push the ends of the stub wire through the moss and then bend them back and tuck them into the underside of the wreath to anchor the fruit. Attach three groups of five lemons in this way, arranging the groups an equal distance from one another.

5 Using the same technique as described in step 4, add three groups of wired-up oranges and three groups of wired-up limes to the wreath.

6 Cut the fruiting ivy sprigs to 15 cm (6 in) and make up small bunches of three to five stems. To wire the bunches, bend a medium-gauge stub wire into a hairpin shape with one leg longer than the other. Hold the U-end against the stems and wrap the long leg of wire around the stems and the other leg of wire, then bring the wires together. Wire up at least 80 sprays.

7 Lastly, add the sprays of wired-up fruiting ivy to the display. Use the foliage to fill in any gaps between the citrus fruits and to cover up any areas of moss on the wreath that are still exposed.

grape and cherry garland

For summer buffets, a garland of fruit and edible nasturtium flowers around the dessert table makes a fresh and colourful addition. Dainty garlands such as this can be simply constructed on a thin gold cord and pinned to the tablecloth. First wash the materials, especially nasturtiums, to ensure that they are bug free.

MATERIALS & EQUIPMENT

the length of rope and quantity of fruit, nasturtiums and ivy will depend on the size of your chosen table; for a table 60 cm (24 in) in diameter allow:

approximately 2.5 m (2¾ yds) gold cord, 1 cm (½ in) diameter

5 strands trailing ivy (*Hedera*), 50 cm (20 in) long

1 kg (2½ lb) green and black grapes

1 kg (2½ lb) cherries

6 punnets edible nasturtiums (*Tropaeolum*)

florist's scissors • florist's tape

pearl-headed haberdashery pins • medium-gauge stub wires

1 Work out exactly how much gold cord you need to make the garland by taking the cord around the table edge. Cut the cord to length and then start the garland by twisting a strand of trailing ivy around the gold cord.

2 Bind the first stem end of trailing ivy to the gold cord with florist's tape. This will hold the stem in place and seal it, preventing it from drying out. Use florist's tape to join more strands of ivy to one another and to bind them to the gold cord until the cord is covered with ivy.

3 When you have woven and bound the ends of the ivy with florist's tape, use the pearl-headed pins to attach the gold cord securely to the edge of the tablecloth so that it can carry the weight of the fruit and flowers without sagging. Make sure that the decorative pinheads are visible at the top edge. Work your way around the table, pinning the cord to the cloth at intervals of about 20 cm (8 in).

4 Next, wire up bunches of grapes and cherries on double-leg mounts using medium-gauge stub wires. To do this, bend a wire into a U-shape, creating a long and a short end. Place the shorter end of wire against the fruit stems and wrap the longer leg of wire around the stems three times. Then bring the two ends together.

5 Attach bunches of grapes to the garland every 20 cm (8 in). Thread the stub wires through the cord from the top edge of the table. Twist the wires around the cord and then flop the bunches of grapes over so that they hang down. Then hide the stub wires by carefully repositioning the ivy leaves. Alternate the bunches of black and green grapes.

6 When you have wired the bunches of grapes around the entire garland, begin attaching groups of cherries. Use the same technique as described in step 5, but place the cherries between the bunches of grapes. Again, cover the wires under ivy leaves.

7 When all the cherries are secure, finish off the garland with nasturtium flowers. Trim the flower stems to 5 cm (2 in) and simply tuck each thin, curved stem behind the cord and it will stay in place. Tuck the flowers behind the cord from both the top and bottom edge; this will ensure that the flowers will face in different directions.

aubergine and orchid wreath

The striking contrast of deep burgundy aubergines and painter's palettes set against vivid yellow pattypan squashes and yarrow produces a richly exotic table display. The flowers and foliage are grouped together for maximum visual impact and interwoven with swirls of stephanandra vine to create movement.

MATERIALS & EQUIPMENT

circular wire frame, 45 cm (18 in) diameter

sphagnum moss

9 painter's palettes (*Anthurium*)

30 baby aubergines

2 stems stephanandra vine (*Stephanandra tanakae*), 1 m (3 ft) long, leaves removed and reserved

10 sprays yellow yarrow (*Achillea* 'Moonshine')

15 orchids (*Cymbidium*) • 30 yellow pattypan squash

reel wire • wire cutters • florist's scissors

german pins • heavy-gauge stub wires • medium-gauge stub wires

1 Cover the wire frame with clumps of damp moss. As you place the moss on the base, wind reel wire tightly around it to secure the moss to the frame. Next, using florist's scissors, trim away any straggly pieces so that the moss sits neatly against the circular wire frame.

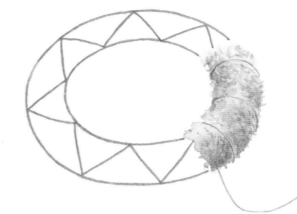

2 Soak the stems of the painter's palettes in water, then cut them to 10 cm (4 in). Wire up the flowers using a medium-gauge stub wire bent into a hairpin shape with one leg longer than the other. Hold the U-end against a stem. Wrap the long leg of wire around the stem and the other leg, then pull the two wires together. Insert three groups of two flowers equidistant from one another on the wreath. Place each pair back to back.

3 Build up the rest of the display around the painter's palettes. Wire up each aubergine by threading a heavy-gauge stub wire through the skin and then twisting the two ends together. Arrange ten aubergines in a fan shape around the painter's palettes. To secure the aubergines, push the wires into the moss and turn each wire back on itself.

4 Next, wire up each vine leaf and each stem of yellow yarrow. Use a double-leg mount as described in step 2. Fill any spaces between the flowers and aubergines with the leaves. Then, working out from the three groups of flowers and vegetables, fill in the wreath base with yarrow.

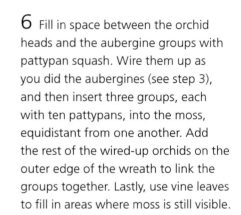

5 Insert a wired-up painter's palette next to the yarrow on the outer edge. Next, wire up each orchid head on a medium-gauge stub wire using a double-leg mount as described in step 2. Arrange half the wired orchid heads in tight groups on the inner edge of the wreath.

6 Fill in space between the orchid heads and the aubergine groups with pattypan squash. Wire them up as you did the aubergines (see step 3), and then insert three groups, each with ten pattypans, into the moss, equidistant from one another. Add the rest of the wired-up orchids on the outer edge of the wreath to link the groups together. Lastly, use vine leaves to fill in areas where moss is still visible.

7 Using medium-gauge stub wire, double-leg mount one end of a length of vine as described in step 2. Push the wires through the moss base of the wreath to hold the vine in place. Wrap the vine loosely around the flowers and vegetables in a series of decorative loops. To finish off, double-leg mount the other end of the vine and push the wires into the base. Repeat this step for the second length of vine.

ABOVE A hand-tied posy adds the finishing touch to a church event. Soft green lady's mantle and pink hydrangeas are mixed with deep red peonies, cockscomb and 'Black Velvet' roses. The flowers were threaded through an iron ring candle holder on the cross to hold them in place.

ABOVE Constructed out of garden canes held together with reel wire, this eye-catching gold star is covered in hundreds of tiny oak leaves, each of which has been dried, sprayed gold and then glued onto the garden canes. Hide the framework by tightly overlapping the oak leaves.

ABOVE Ivy and butcher's broom foliage are mixed with lilac, hyacinths, ranunculi and bell-shaped campanula spires to produce a fragrant display. A fresh floral foam dome, which clips onto the arm of the church pew end, forms the foundation for this diamond-shaped arrangement.

celebrations

Since ancient Greek and Roman times, people have chosen wreaths and garlands to celebrate great events. The Greeks crowned the winners of their poetic and athletic competitions with garlands of fresh laurel, oak and olive leaves, while the Romans chose head wreaths to honour their great military heroes. What better way to mark a special occasion, whether it is Valentine's Day, Christmas, or an important anniversary, than by following in this grand tradition and creating a memorable display of flowers or foliage?

ABOVE As a token of your love on Valentine's Day, soften red dogwood stems by soaking them in warm water and bend them into a heart. Secure the shape with red ribbon and add three stems of beautiful 'Grand Prix' roses.

RIGHT A dazzling display for a golden wedding anniversary celebration has been created by packing a heart-shaped frame with damp moss and covering it in a background of soft lilac and pale green hydrangeas, topped with stunning yellow 'Sultan' gerberas and 'Golden Gate' roses.

ABOVE A spectacular Christmas wreath is created using a whorl of birch twigs dipped in red paint and sprinkled with glitter. To shape them into a ring, cut the stems to 7.5 cm (3 in) long and bind groups of birch twigs to one another with reel wire. Bend the twigs into a circle as you work until the ring is complete. Thread tiny 'pea' lights through the birch at the back of the wreath to make the display sparkle, and hide the electric wire from view with more twigs.

LEFT A hanging festive wreath of bright flowers and candles is built up from a wire-frame foundation covered in moss. The candles and curls of ribbon are then attached to the base with heavy-gauge stub wires before the display is hung. Once in place, fruiting ivy and sea holly form a bed of foliage for vivid marigolds, 'Jaguar' roses, ranunculi and anemones.

bridal headdress

This dainty spring headdress looks charming on young brides, small
bridesmaids, or girls taking their First Holy Communion. Constructed
on a fine wire frame so that it is light to wear, it can be tailor-made so that
it fits comfortably. The flowers and foliage, including delicate lily-of-the-valley
flowers, hyacinth florets, purple-edged ranunculi and small-leaved ivy, come
together to impart a deliciously subtle fragrance.

MATERIALS & EQUIPMENT

15 sprigs ivy (*Hedera*), plus individual leaves

11 lilies-of-the-valley (*Convallaria majalis*)

15 blue hyacinths (*Hyacinthus*)

15 fritillaries (*Fritillaria pinardii*)

16 blue cornflowers (*Centaurea cyanus*)

10 white lisianthus (*Eustoma grandiflorum*)

11 variegated ranunculi (*Ranunculus* 'Cappuccino')

fine-gauge stub wires • silver wire • wire cutters • florist's tape

large circular tin • medium-gauge stub wires • florist's scissors • pliers

1 Condition the cut flowers and foliage in water for up to 12 hours. Meanwhile, create the wire framework for the headdress. Using silver wire, join up two fine-gauge stub wires. Bind the length of wire in florist's tape.

2 Using a large tin as a mould, bend the wire into a circle and check that it fits the wearer. Hook both the ends to make a clasp.

3 Wire up individual ivy leaves to use later to cover the hooks at each end of the headdress. To do this, stitch a fine-gauge stub wire through the midrib of each ivy leaf. Pull the wire ends down and twist them together. Bind the wire and leaf base with florist's tape to seal in the leaf moisture and form a stem.

4 Next, wire up delicate sprigs of ivy and lilies-of-the-valley to provide their stems with support. Cut each stem to 10 cm (4 in) and wind a medium-gauge stub wire along its length, taking care to avoid the ivy leaves or lily-of-the-valley florets themselves. Bind the wire with florist's tape.

5 Wire up the hyacinths next. Cut off florets from the flower. Push a medium-gauge stub wire up through the base of the floret, and make a hook. Pull the wire back down inside the floret to anchor the hook. Thread a silver wire crossways through the bottom third of the floret. Pinch the wires together and bind with florist's tape. Wire up fritillaries and cornflowers using this method.

6 Now wire up the fatter-stemmed lisianthus and ranunculi. To do this, cut off most of the stem, leaving 1 cm (½ in). Push a medium-gauge stub wire up through the stem and flower until it reaches the calyx in the lower third of the flower head. Insert a silver wire crossways through the stem, making one end longer than the other. Pinch the wires together and wind the longer length of silver wire around the stem a few times. Bind the wires and short stem with florist's tape.

7 Lay out the flowers and foliage on your work surface according to type; this will make wiring them to the framework easier. Straighten out the frame; hide the clasp by placing an ivy leaf against it. Bind on the leaf with florist's tape.

8 Bind on more flowers and foliage with florist's tape to build up the headdress. Add lilies-of-the-valley followed by cornflowers, ranunculi, ivy sprigs, hyacinth florets and lisianthus. Add the smaller flowers in groups so that they can be seen and larger flowers in twos or threes. Trim the stems as you work.

9 After the lisianthus, bind in ivy leaves, then fritillaries; then begin the sequence again from step 8. Allow the stems to overlap so that the headdress looks full. Lastly, cover the clasp in an ivy leaf as described in step 7. To finish off, bind the tape around the wire end and cut.

10 Finally, bend the wreath back into a circle. Spray-mist the wreath with water to keep it fresh and pinch the clasp together with pliers to hold the headdress in place.

heart-shaped table centrepiece

Tall displays of flowers and foliage, either incorporated on a candelabra
or, as here, elevated on a pole, have become increasingly fashionable
for the guest tables at weddings. Not only do they make a theatrical
impact in a large room, they allow guests to witness the speeches
without anything obstructing their view.

MATERIALS & EQUIPMENT

stone urn, 45 cm (18 in) high, 30 cm (12 in) diameter

2 blocks floral foam, 20 x 10 x 8 cm (8 x 4 x 3 in)

heart-shaped twig wreath, 25 cm (10 in) across at widest point • sphagnum moss

2.5-cm (1-in) chicken wire, 100 x 30 cm (40 x 12 in) • wooden pole, 80 cm (32 in) long

15 sprigs beech foliage (*Fagus*) • 15 sprigs lady's mantle (*Alchemilla mollis*)

15 sprigs pittosporum (*Pittosporum*) • 15 sprigs guelder rose (*Viburnum opulus*)

13 mauve hydrangeas (*Hydrangea*) • 14 blue scabious (*Scabiosa*)

16 pink lisianthus (*Eustoma grandiflorum*) • 15 pale pink roses (*Rosa* 'Delilah')

strand of ivy (*Hedera*), approximately 80 cm (32 in) long

plastic bin liner • florist's knife • florist's tape • florist's scissors

wire cutters • reel wire • heavy-gauge stub wire

1 Line the urn with a plastic bin liner and then wedge two pre-soaked blocks of floral foam into it. For a good fit, trim down the two sides of the foam blocks with a florist's knife.

2 Tape the wet foam blocks in place using waterproof florist's tape. Next, trim the top edge of the bin liner so that it sits neatly inside the urn.

3 Working from the outer edges of the urn to the centre, build up a mound shape of foliage using sprigs of beech, lady's mantle, pittosporum and guelder rose. For the outer edges, cut 25 cm (10 in) sprigs and insert them upside-down so that they trail over the edges. Use the shorter lengths to fill in the centre.

4 When the foam is covered with foliage, add the flowers, starting with the hydrangea heads. Cut the stems to 20 cm (8 in) and, following the mound shape of foliage, distribute the shapes and colours of the flowers evenly as the display will be viewed from all sides.

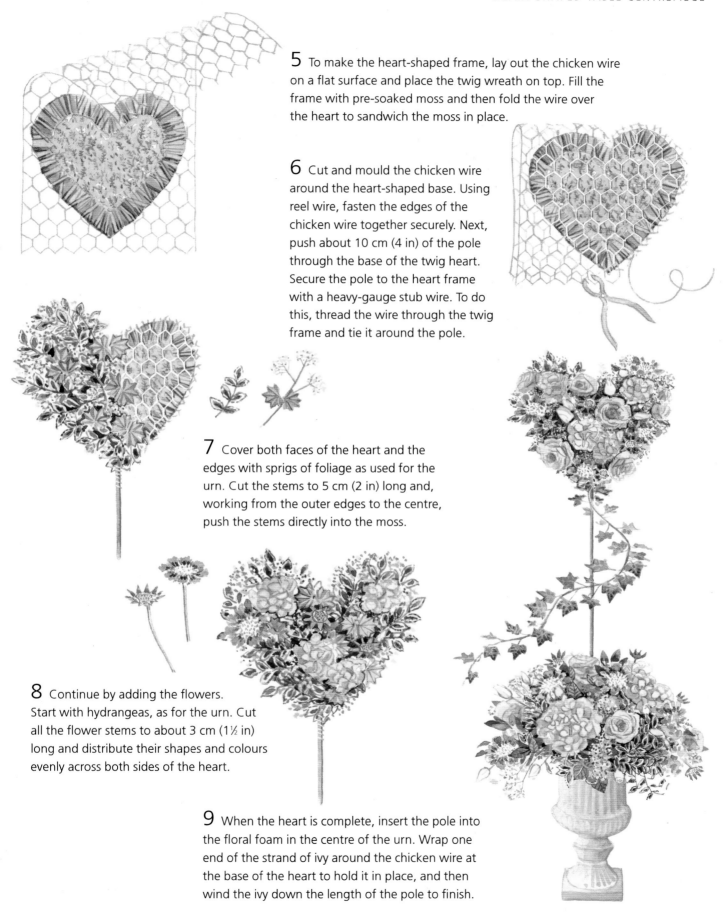

5 To make the heart-shaped frame, lay out the chicken wire on a flat surface and place the twig wreath on top. Fill the frame with pre-soaked moss and then fold the wire over the heart to sandwich the moss in place.

6 Cut and mould the chicken wire around the heart-shaped base. Using reel wire, fasten the edges of the chicken wire together securely. Next, push about 10 cm (4 in) of the pole through the base of the twig heart. Secure the pole to the heart frame with a heavy-gauge stub wire. To do this, thread the wire through the twig frame and tie it around the pole.

7 Cover both faces of the heart and the edges with sprigs of foliage as used for the urn. Cut the stems to 5 cm (2 in) long and, working from the outer edges to the centre, push the stems directly into the moss.

8 Continue by adding the flowers. Start with hydrangeas, as for the urn. Cut all the flower stems to about 3 cm (1½ in) long and distribute their shapes and colours evenly across both sides of the heart.

9 When the heart is complete, insert the pole into the floral foam in the centre of the urn. Wrap one end of the strand of ivy around the chicken wire at the base of the heart to hold it in place, and then wind the ivy down the length of the pole to finish.

chair-back decoration

This simple hand-tied swag of scented pink roses and rich purple lisianthus is easy to make and looks stunning. Use a generous length of brightly coloured satin ribbon to attach the swag flamboyantly to the back of the chair where a guest of honour will sit, or make several to decorate the aisle seats at a wedding.

MATERIALS & EQUIPMENT

1 m (1 yd) raffia

5 stems viburnum (*Viburnum tinus*)

16 deep pink roses (*Rosa* 'Martinez')

9 pale pink roses (*Rosa* 'Delilah')

4 cockscomb (*Celosia argentea*)

18 purple lisianthus (*Eustoma grandiflorum*)

3.5 m (4 yds) cerise ribbon, 5 cm (2 in) wide

florist's scissors

1 Cut the viburnum stems to 40 cm (16 in). To form the foundation of this display, hold one stem of foliage upright and then criss-cross another stem behind (to the right) and a third in front (to the left). Bind the stems together with raffia.

2 Add two more stems of viburnum, criss-crossing one behind and one in front. Pull the stems down into the display to fill in any gaps; remember that you are trying to create a diamond shape. When the viburnum stems are in place, bind them into the bunch with raffia. Trim the stems to 20 cm (8 in).

3 Next add the 'Martinez' roses. Take three stems about 60 cm (24 in) long, and arrange them behind the viburnum. Stand one rose in the centre and tilt one to the left and one to the right. Tie the rose stems to the viburnum at the centre point with raffia.

4 Continue building up the tied bunch by adding two more 'Martinez' roses. Thread the stems at an angle through the viburnum and pull the rose heads down into the display to fill in the diamond shape. Tie the rose stems with raffia and trim them to the same length as the viburnum stems.

5 Continue weaving and binding the 'Martinez' roses into the bouquet, criss-crossing the flowers through the tied bunch to obtain an even distribution of colour. Next, add the 'Delilah' roses using the same criss-cross technique. Trim the stems to one length.

6 Next, add the stems of cockscomb to fill in any obvious gaps between the roses and viburnum. Lastly, add long stems of purple lisianthus to the front and back of the bouquet. Tie the flower stems in place with raffia and trim down the lisianthus and cockscomb stems to the same length as those of the roses and viburnum.

7 To make the bow, cut two pieces of ribbon 50 cm (20 in) long. Fold one piece into three loops and pinch the loops together in the middle. Take the second ribbon and tie it in a single knot around the centre of the loops.

8 Lastly, tie the bouquet to the back of the chair with a 2-m (2-yd) length of ribbon. When it is secure, fasten the bow onto the bouquet using the short ribbon tails of the bow.

banister garland

Create a grand staircase for your guests by constructing an abundant
garland of fresh flowers and foliage on a floral foam base. The foam foundation
can be bought in standard lengths from specialist florists and joined together
to achieve the desired length. Pre-soak the foam base to keep the fresh
materials well watered, and take care to fasten the garland securely to
the banister as the finished display will be very heavy.

MATERIALS & EQUIPMENT

floral foam garland, available in 2 m (6 ft) lengths, composed of 14.5 cm (6 in) sections;
for each 14.5 cm (6 in) section of floral foam allow approximately:

20 sprigs of senecio (*Senecio cineraria*)

4 sprays green double lisianthus (*Eustoma grandiflorum*)

4 sprays pink double lisianthus (*Eustoma grandiflorum*)

2 white tuberoses (*Polianthes tuberosa*)

2–3 cream roses (*Rosa* 'Anna')

10 sprigs snowberry (*Symphoricarpos*)

1 m (1 yd) silk ribbon, 4 cm (1¾ in) wide

plastic sheets • florist's scissors

reel wire • wire cutters

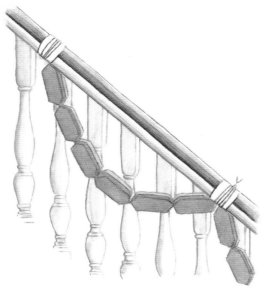

1 Soak each section of the foam garland in water for five minutes. Meanwhile, cover the stairs with plastic sheets. Then, protect the wooden handrail. To do this, bind lengths of ribbon around the rail at the points where you intend to attach the garland. Using reel wire, bind the pre-soaked garland to the handrail on top of the protective ribbon. Secure every sixth section of foam using this technique.

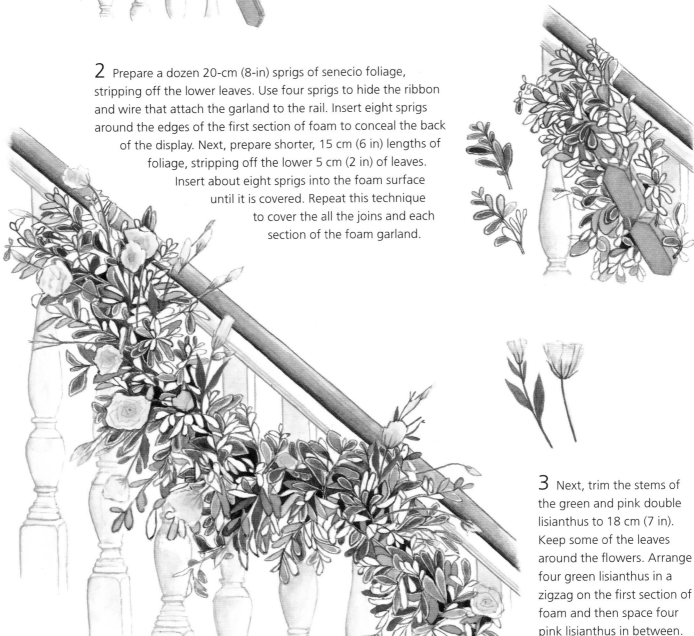

2 Prepare a dozen 20-cm (8-in) sprigs of senecio foliage, stripping off the lower leaves. Use four sprigs to hide the ribbon and wire that attach the garland to the rail. Insert eight sprigs around the edges of the first section of foam to conceal the back of the display. Next, prepare shorter, 15 cm (6 in) lengths of foliage, stripping off the lower 5 cm (2 in) of leaves. Insert about eight sprigs into the foam surface until it is covered. Repeat this technique to cover the all the joins and each section of the foam garland.

3 Next, trim the stems of the green and pink double lisianthus to 18 cm (7 in). Keep some of the leaves around the flowers. Arrange four green lisianthus in a zigzag on the first section of foam and then space four pink lisianthus in between. Repeat this step for each section of the garland.

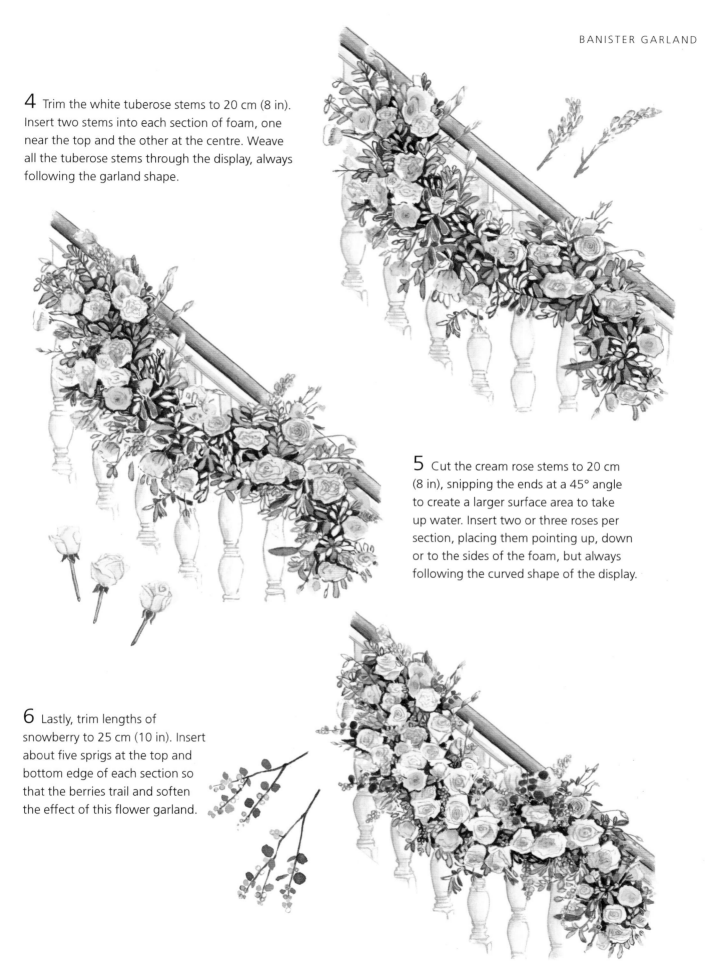

4 Trim the white tuberose stems to 20 cm (8 in). Insert two stems into each section of foam, one near the top and the other at the centre. Weave all the tuberose stems through the display, always following the garland shape.

5 Cut the cream rose stems to 20 cm (8 in), snipping the ends at a 45° angle to create a larger surface area to take up water. Insert two or three roses per section, placing them pointing up, down or to the sides of the foam, but always following the curved shape of the display.

6 Lastly, trim lengths of snowberry to 25 cm (10 in). Insert about five sprigs at the top and bottom edge of each section so that the berries trail and soften the effect of this flower garland.

wreath materials

Wreath frames can be purchased from good florists, garden centres and specialist floristry suppliers and are available in an extraordinary variety of shapes and sizes. Made from natural materials, such as flexible dogwood stems, honeysuckle, or clematis vine, and bound together with reel wire or garden string, these simple rigid foundations form the building blocks of fresh or dried flower displays.

A shop-bought wreath base is always a worthwhile investment because, unlike fresh floral foam bases, they can be reused again and again. However, if you want to create a particular shape it may be simpler and more cost-effective to create your own base. Amateur gardeners or enthusiastic walkers can collect plant stems and trailing vines from the garden or countryside to fashion into wreath bases. Select any pliable woody stems and try to harvest these branches in spring before the sap rises, or

in autumn after the sap has fallen. Dogwood, corkscrew hazel and birch are my favourite woods and honeysuckle, kiwi, wisteria and grape are my favourite garden vines but you can also find clematis and honeysuckle in the wild. If the twigs or vines are dry, soak them in warm water until they become more flexible and easier to work with. Start by picking out a few long stems and gently ease them into a circle. If the stems are too short, keep adding new lengths by staggering and overlapping stems until you have a circle. Bind the stems tightly with reel wire to keep the twigs in place. If you are confident when the stems are dry that they have taken on the right shape, take off the wire.

WIRE FRAMES

Rigid wire wreath frames can be purchased ready-made in a bewildering number of dimensions. There is little standardization for popular shapes, such as crosses, circles and stars, because manufacturers from different countries have their own sizing systems, based largely around their funeral wreath traditions.

If you cannot buy the size or shape of frame you require, you could try making your own, but bear in mind that it may be difficult to buy materials such as stub wires, reel wire and other sundries in small quantities. Most florists will carry a limited stock but they may be reluctant to sell them to the public and they may have to order them especially from wholesalers. For a more 'do-it-yourself' approach, try moulding wire coat hangers into simple frames or folding chicken wire around a strip of damp moss and bending it into a shape. Of course, medium-gauge stub wires and silver wire form the underlying structure for bridal headdresses, but for sturdier metal-framed structures, you could commission a metal worker to solder iron into the required shapes.

Wire frames are more permanent than either twig or foam bases and can be used again and again. Often damp moss is attached to the bare wire frame with reel wire to form a moist bed for fresh flowers. If the moss is very damp, the back of the wire wreath can be lined with plastic to protect the surface.

LARGE-SCALE DESIGNS

Wire frames are ideally suited to particularly large and heavy displays. When designs on a grand scale are needed, two wire frames can be bound together with reel wire to reinforce the structure; for example, sturdy wire frames are used to support a large nautical-theme wreath constructed out of twists of rope and shells (see p. 12) and a heavy frame of driftwood (see p. 28).

FLORAL FOAM BASES

Fresh floral foam is green, and dry foam is either brown or grey. Both types of foam come in blocks or specially moulded shapes; fresh foam is soaked in water before use to prolong the life of the flowers and foliage. Inserting stems into moist foam will help plant materials stay fresh for longer, although they will not last as long as they would if arranged in a vase of water. Although fresh floral foam bases are simple to work with, they are really suitable only for short-term hanging decorations because as the foam dries out and contracts, the plant material becomes dislodged and drops out. For this reason, foam shapes are best used for table centrepieces; the foam sits in a plastic base that protects the table surface. When soaking fresh floral foam blocks in water, allow the foam to sink gradually. When air bubbles no longer rise to the surface, it is ready for use. Bear in mind that fresh foam can be used only for one display as it will take up water effectively only on its first soak.

Although there are only a few floral foam manufacturers, the styles and shapes of the foam products they offer vary enormously. Even good florists and garden centres hold only limited stock but you can select the size and dimensions you wish by ordering supplies from mail-order catalogues. In addition to round ring frames, balls, cones and open-heart shapes, there are flat designer boards that can be cut into any shape. Also, specialist foam designs can be purchased for keeping fresh flowers and foliage alive on twig and wire wreaths. One type, known as 'Le Bump™', consists of a small block of dome-shaped floral foam with a screw-in base. Another type, known as 'Le Klip™', designed to attach flower displays to church pews, consists of a similar dome of fresh floral foam held in a plastic cage and with a removable attachment that clips on to the end of the pew.

FLEXIBLE BASES

Flexible foam bases, which can be draped along a banister, are also available for creating garlands out of delicate plant materials that require a constant supply of water. These specially manufactured bases can be bought in 2 m (6 ft) lengths and must be soaked thoroughly in water before use.

equipment & techniques

WREATH-MAKING EQUIPMENT

A flat, non-scratch work surface that stands at a suitable height so that the user does not have to stoop is the first piece of equipment needed when wreath-making. It is also useful when creating hanging wreaths to have a place where you can hang the display so that you can check how the finished arrangement will look. Scrap paper on the work surface and dust sheets on the floor are also essential, especially when you are working on a display on location. Opt for plastic rather than fabric dust sheets to prevent moisture from seeping through to the floor below. When you have finished, you can simply fold up the ground sheets to clear away any waste plant material quickly.

ESSENTIAL TOOLS

Floristry scissors and secateurs are essential for collecting fresh plant materials and trimming down stems. A small florist's knife is handy for stripping the lower leaves from plant stems and for trimming blocks of floral foam to the required shape. Wire cutters are required for cutting chicken wire, stub wires and reel wire, and pliers are also useful. A glue gun is an indispensable tool for those who enjoy attaching unusual or heavy items, such as shells and wood, to wreaths, but should be used with care. The hot liquid glue sticks most materals, including wet items and dry porous objects, and it saves time, as it takes only a few seconds for the glue to dry. Both high- and low-temperature guns are available; low-temperature guns are more suitable for attaching fresh plant material. Waterproof florist's tape is also useful for anchoring wet foam in containers, as is gutta-percha tape, which seals moisture within plant stems.

CONDITIONING PLANTS

The most recent research recommends the following simple guidelines for conditioning fresh flowers and foliage before they are arranged on a wreath. If you follow these measures and condition

flowers and foliage for several hours or overnight, they will last longer in the finished display. As a general rule, take at least 3 cm (1¼ in) off the bottom of the plant stem and make a slanted cut with a sharp florist's knife to expose the maximum surface area to water, rather than smashing or splitting the base of the stem. Next, remove the lower leaves from the plant stems, because leaves submerged under water may rot and produce bacteria that will shorten the life of the plant material. Before placing the cut flowers and foliage in a container for conditioning, make sure that it is scrupulously clean and fill it with lukewarm water, mixed with flower food. The food will feed the flowers, and will prevent bacteria from growing.

PROTECTING SURFACES

It is a good idea to protect doors, walls and tables, or any other surfaces or items of furniture in the home that may come into contact with water or moisture from fresh flower wreaths. Water is particularly harmful to unprotected wood finishes and can leave marks that are difficult to remove or cause the wood to warp. For small table wreaths, simply place a waterproof table mat or piece of thick felt under the tablecloth, but for grand-scale designs that are too large to sit on a mat, you will have to make your own protective covering out of a waterproof material. The best method is to cut a plastic bin liner into long thin strips and fasten the strips to the back of the wreath base with german pins or small U-shaped pins to prevent any moisture from penetrating the furniture or wall.

Pin several strips of plastic over the damp moss covering the wreath base to prevent any water seepage.

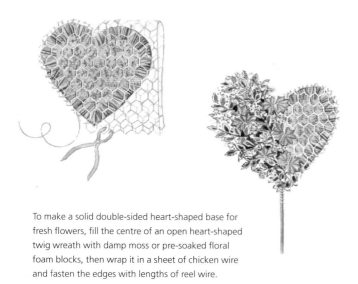

To make a solid double-sided heart-shaped base for fresh flowers, fill the centre of an open heart-shaped twig wreath with damp moss or pre-soaked floral foam blocks, then wrap it in a sheet of chicken wire and fasten the edges with lengths of reel wire.

DRYING YOUR OWN MATERIALS

If you wish to create more permanent wreaths, buy bunches of dried materials, such as roses and glycerined beech leaves, from a good florist, or try harvesting and drying your own materials, such as bunches of lavender from the garden. In recent years there have been great improvements in the quality of shop-bought dried flowers available, mainly due to new techniques for freeze-drying flower heads, particularly roses. These new methods have produced amazingly life-like flowers, whose petals maintain their natural beauty and suppleness. However, displays using freeze-dried flowers must be kept away from moist conditions, such as those found in bathrooms or kitchens, because the flowers tend to absorb moisture from the air and deteriorate rapidly.

You can easily dry your own plant materials for wreath-making. The simplest way to is to hang them upside-down in bunches and store them in a cool, dark, dry room. Although warm, the conditions in an airing cupboard are some of the best found

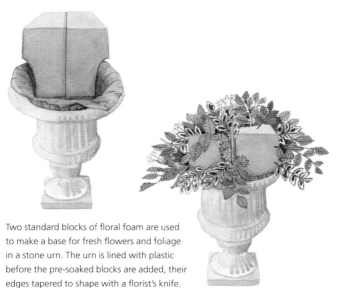

Two standard blocks of floral foam are used to make a base for fresh flowers and foliage in a stone urn. The urn is lined with plastic before the pre-soaked blocks are added, their edges tapered to shape with a florist's knife.

within the home; the warm air will dry plant materials quickly, but with a small degree of colour fading. When the materials are thoroughly dry, store them in large cardboard boxes or paper bags. Make sure that the flowers or leaves do not touch one another and place them between layers of tissue paper to avoid damaging the plant material. Avoid using plastic bags to store plant material as they may become moist, which will cause the dried flowers and leaves to deteriorate.

ADAPTING WREATH BASES

If you cannot find the exact wreath base for your project, adapt the materials you have at your disposal and make your own. For example, if you want to create a heart of fresh flowers, fill an exisiting heart-shaped twig frame with damp moss or blocks of pre-soaked floral foam and use chicken wire to sandwich the moss or foam within the frame. Remember, it is possible to cut or trim most materials to shape to suit your needs. For example,

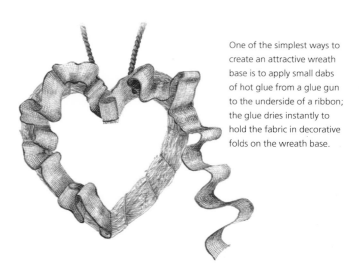

One of the simplest ways to create an attractive wreath base is to apply small dabs of hot glue from a glue gun to the underside of a ribbon; the glue dries instantly to hold the fabric in decorative folds on the wreath base.

pre-soaked floral foam can be tapered to fit any container and then held in place with florist's tape, and flat designer board can be cut into a letter or number, using a template as a guide. Twig and dry foam bases are even more versatile than floral foam and form the foundation for many wreath displays; they can be used time and again to different effect. A twig frame makes a good starting point for a fabric wreath – wrap the frame in quilting material to create a padded effect, then cover it in the fabric of your choice. Alternatively, natural wreath bases can be customized by coating with spray paint.

ATTACHING MATERIALS TO WREATH BASES

The stems of fresh flowers and foliage are easy to insert in a fresh foam base but there are several tried-and-tested techniques for attaching materials to dry foam or twig bases. Objects such as ribbon and shells are best glued to the base using a hot glue gun or strong adhesive, while groups of decorative items, such as dried fruits and cherubs, should be wired to the wreath or pinned securely in place.

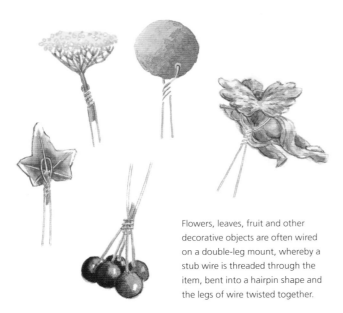

Flowers, leaves, fruit and other decorative objects are often wired on a double-leg mount, whereby a stub wire is threaded through the item, bent into a hairpin shape and the legs of wire twisted together.

SUPPORTS

Wire is essential in wreath-making for holding the structure together, for anchoring a bed of moss to the wreath base and for attaching decorative plant materials, fruits, objects and ribbon bows. The two main types of wire used are florist's stub wire and reel wire. Florist's stub wire comes in a bewildering number of thicknesses and lengths, and its primary function is to reinforce the plant stem. As a general guideline, use fine-gauge stub wire to support delicate flowers and leaves and also to wire up individual florets in bridal work. Medium-gauge stub wire is used to support medium-sized flowers and decorative objects, while heavy-gauge stub wires are reserved for large or heavy flower heads or to create a hook from which to hang the finished wreath. Reel wire is useful for all kinds of binding work. It is used to bind flexible twigs and vines into wreath frames, to attach moss and heavy decorative items, such as rope and wood, onto shop-bought frames, and to bind individual stems and bunches of flowers and foliage onto a length of rope to make a garland. In addition to using stub wires or reel wire, you can also use U-shaped, or german pins, to fasten materials to a wreath base. These work particularly well if you want an item to sit flush with the frame, for example clumps of carpet moss or branches of pine, or when you are attaching a waterproof backing to a wreath. Either buy german pins from specialist suppliers, which can be very expensive, or make your own by cutting heavy-gauge stub wires into short lengths and bending them into shape with pliers. In addition to attaching plant materials with wires, you can also use pearl-headed haberdashery pins to fasten garlands of flowers and trailing stems of ivy and fresh fruits to tablecloths for special celebrations.

USING ROPE, RIBBON OR RAFFIA

The great choice of colourful ropes, ribbons and raffias available to the wreath-maker is inspiring and these materials will add the finishing creative touch to any display. Use your imagination to explore their use on wreaths and experiment by attaching pleated folds of pretty ribbon to a wreath base with a hot glue gun or pinning a length of luxurious velvet or silk ribbon to a wreath frame to make a decorative hanging for the display. Alternatively, attach the ribbon after all the other materials have been added, wrapping trails of ribbon around the flowers and foliage, and finishing off with a bow. Colourful paper raffia can also be used to bind together hand-tied swags of flower stems that are then attached to a chair back with a generous length of ribbon and finished with a double bow.

MAINTAINING THE FINISHED WREATH

Once you have created your wreath, garland or swag of fresh flowers and foliage, keep it looking its best by spray-misting the plant materials and moss base with clean water on a daily basis. If the materials have been conditioned well beforehand, they should last for several days and even up to a week within the display. For arrangements built on a foundation of fresh foam, keep checking that the foam is moist to the touch and add more water only when it starts to dry out. For more long-lasting displays, choose plants that thrive on little water, such as succulents. Fresh displays of this type will last for up to six weeks and are known as living wreaths. To ensure wreaths of dried flowers and foliage stay in good condition, keep them out of moist environments such as kitchens and bathrooms that may cause the plant materials to deteriorate. Try also to keep dried arrangements away from direct heat and sunlight, which makes plant materials fade, and dust them at regular intervals to prevent dust particles from collecting on leaves and petals.

A decorative bow is easy to make: simply fold a ribbon into three loops and pinch the loops together in the middle. Take a second length of ribbon and tie it in a single knot around the centre of the loops.

plant directory

Abies nobilis (blue pine) p. 50
Evergreen trees which have thick
bluish pine needles, branches are
available from late autumn for use
in Christmas garlands and wreaths
but can be bought throughout the
year. The pine needles last well in
displays. Branches should be stored
in the cold, out of water before use.
CARE To condition, cut the stem ends
with secateurs and remove the lower
needles. To avoid shedding needles,
buy food especially for Christmas trees.

Achillea 'Moonshine' (yarrow)
pp. 42, 78
Tall, summer-flowering perennial
with attractive clusters of sulphur-
yellow flowers and an aromatic
fragrance. The dense flower
heads are useful for filling in
arrangements. Cut or purchase
the flowers when they are at
least three-quarters open.
CARE Remove all lower foliage, cut
1 cm (½ in) from the stem base and
soak in a solution of flower food.

Alchemilla mollis (lady's mantle) p. 88
Perennial plant with lime-green
flowers and fan-shaped leaves that
grows to about 40–50 cm (16–20 in)
high. It flowers between early and
late summer. The flowers should be
cut or bought from a florist when
most of the flowers are open.
CARE Cut the stems ends at an angle
and then soak in water before use.

Anemone coronaria (anemone) p. 38
Jewel-coloured flowers in shades
of blue, purple, red and pink with
crowns of leaves around the petals
on a leafless stem. Depending on

the variety, they reach between
25–45 cm (10–18 in) in height.
Available from winter to early
summer, they peak in spring.
CARE These thirsty flowers require
no special treatment. Simply cut the
stems ends at an angle and soak in
water before use.

Anethum graveolens (dill) p. 42
A strongly aromatic herb with
feathery flowers which are
excellent fillers in arrangements.
Cut or purchase when the main
umbel is fully grown.
CARE To condition, cut the stem ends
at an angle, remove lower foliage, and
place in clean water with flower food.

Anthurium (painter's palette) p. 78
A tropical plant originating from
the rainforests of Colombia, it is
prized for its waxy green leaves
and brightly coloured or pale
heart-shaped flowers. The flowers
must be mature on purchase
and will last for up to three
weeks or more.
CARE Cut the stem ends and soak in
fresh water and flower food. Store out
of the cold, which will cause the
flowers to discolour.

Capsicum (chilli pepper) p. 42
Chilli seeds germinate in spring
and by summer the plants produce
shiny red or green fruits. Sold as
vegetables for most of the year,
dried chilli peppers on stems are
available in autumn and winter.
They are very useful for adding
colour and texture to festive
wreaths and garlands.
CARE No special care instructions.

Celosia argentea (cockscomb) p. 92
Originally from tropical Africa,
this flowering plant comes in two
forms which have either crests
or plumes of brilliant deep red,
magenta-pink or gold flowers.
CARE Trim the stem ends at an angle
and condition with flower food.
Remove all foliage.

Centaurea cyanus (cornflower) p. 84
There are many cornflowers in this
family but the best known are the
bright blue annuals with ruffled
petals, which are available from
spring to autumn.
CARE Remove the foliage, cut the
stems ends at an angle and place in
clean water with flower food.

Clematis vitalba (clematis vine) p. 60
Available in autumn and winter
when the clematis leaves have died
back, leaving a vine stem. This vine
is ideal for making wreath bases
and for wrapping around wreaths
and garlands. Collect from
hedgerows or purchase from
specialist florists.
CARE No special care instructions.

Convallaria majalis
(lily-of-the-valley) p. 84
These sweet-scented, bell-shaped
white flowers are available in late
spring but although they can be
bought throughout the year, they
are expensive.
CARE Trim the stem ends and place
them in water. Do not allow the stems
to dry out in the arrangement.

Cymbidium (cymbidium orchid) p. 78
These popular orchids have waxy

flowers in white, yellow, green or
pink, on long or short stems.
CARE Cut 1 cm (½ in) off the stem and
place in tepid water with flower food.
Do not place the flowers in direct
sunlight or draughts.

Delphinium 'Blue Bees'
(delphinium) p. 38
A perennial with tall stems carrying
spikes of bell-shaped blue flowers.
This variety is often treated before
harvesting to ensure that it keeps
its flowers for up to ten days.
CARE Cut the stems and condition
with flower food.

Echeveria (succulent) p. 20
These rosette-shaped succulents
originate from Mexico and there
are more than 150 species sold as
house and garden plants. They can
survive for weeks in living wreaths
as they require little in the way of
water or nutrients.
CARE Keep the root system intact
when lifting from plant pots.

Eustoma grandiflorum (lisianthus)
pp. 84, 88, 92, 96
These white or blue bell-shaped
flowers are arranged on long stems
as individual blooms or in panicles.
CARE Cut stem ends and condition in
fresh water.

Fagus (beech) pp. 46, 88
An attractive green and copper
foliage which is most spectacular
in autumn when the leaves turn
a much deeper rust colour.
CARE Preserve the leaves in a solution
of glycerine so they can be used in
displays throughout the year.

Fritillaria pinardii (fritillary) p. 84
Delicate, bell-shaped flowers are held on slender stems, and are available in spring. This is one of the alpine varieties from Turkey, whose petals are gold on the inside and brown outside. Despite its fragile appearance, it survives well as a cut flower.
CARE Cut the stem ends at an angle and condition with flower food.

Galax (galax) p. 16
These glossy green heart-shaped leaves are available throughout the year but turn dark red and mottled in autumn. Most galax leaves are harvested in the Appalachian Mountains of North America, from where they are distributed around the world.
CARE Cut and place the leaves in water before use, or buy them for year-round use preserved in glycerine.

Gardenia (gardenia) p. 60
Plants with glossy dark green leaves and highly scented waxy white flowers with either single or double blooms.
CARE Gardenias are most commonly sold as house plants and should be kept moist at all times with tepid water. Spray-mist the leaves and condition cut flowers with flower food before use.

Hedera (ivy)
pp. 38, 42, 64, 70, 74, 84, 88
This versatile evergreen plant has many uses for the flower arranger. Young ivy produces trails of lobe-shaped leaves, which may be variegated, while mature plants produce flowers and dark berries.
CARE Bunches of fruiting ivy need their stems cut and placing in water for a few hours, while young ivy plants in pots should be conditioned overnight with water and flower food.

Helianthus (sunflower) p. 42
Originally from the southern and western regions of North America, this annual flower, with its many golden yellow petals and large dark centre, has become very fashionable. There are single and double varieties and it comes in a number of other colours besides the commonly known yellow.
CARE Cut stem ends at an angle and condition this thirsty flower in fresh water for several hours or overnight.

Hyacinthus (hyacinth) p. 84
An extremely fragrant plant with spikes of bell-shaped flowers in a number of pastel and strong colours. It is popular as a potted bulb plant and now also as a cut flower. The cut flowers last up to 16 days and each flower stalk can be divided into individual florets and wired into headdresses and bridal bouquets.
CARE Cut stem ends at an angle and wipe off any excess sap.

Hydrangea (hydrangea)
pp. 56, 64, 88
Another useful flower for arrangers is the long-lasting, large-headed hydrangea, available in shades of pink, blue or white.
CARE As cut flowers they last for ten days but need constant spray-misting with water. If the flowers dry out, submerge the flower heads in water.

Lavandula (lavender) p. 16
This densely growing fragrant mauve flowering plant has beautiful silvery stems. It can be hung up in bunches to dry and then stored and used for projects throughout the year.
CARE When using fresh, remove the lower foliage and place the stems in deep water. Change the water frequently and use flower food.

Leucospermum cordifolium
(leucospermum) p. 42
A South African flower commonly known as the pincushion flower because of its large clustered red flower head. It lasts well out of water which makes it a useful flower for grand-scale garlands.
CARE Woody stems should be cut at an angle and placed in fresh water and flower food.

Lilium (lily) p. 64
Large-headed scented lilies such as 'Casablanca' and 'Pompeii' work well in wreaths and garlands as the flowers are long-lasting. To prevent pollen stains when people brush past the display, remove the stamens from the centre of the flower heads once open.
CARE Cut the stem ends and place in water overnight.

Lonicera (honeysuckle vine)
pp. 24, 46, 64
Honeysuckle does not last well as a cut flower. In autumn, once the leaves have died back, the flexible vines can be harvested and used to make wreath bases.
CARE No special care instructions.

Ornithogalum montanum
(starflower) p. 38
This spring-flowering bulb has a leafless stem and long-lasting, greenish-white star-flowers.
CARE Cut stem ends and condition for a few hours before use.

Pittosporum (pittosporum) p. 88
Long-lasting evergreen foliage with small ovate leaves; some varieties are variegated.
CARE Cut stem ends cleanly at an angle, then condition in water as normal.

Polianthes tuberosa (tuberose)
p. 96
Stems of sweetly scented star-shaped cream florets that are popular the world over for bridal arrangements.
CARE Cut stem ends cleanly at an angle, then condition in water for a few hours before arranging.

Ranunculus (ranunculus) pp. 38, 84
These long-lasting and colourful perennials have either single or double blooms and resemble peonies. They are available in winter to late spring.
CARE Cut stems and condition with flower food.

Rosa (rose) pp. 16, 56, 88, 92, 96
There is such a wide variety of roses and new shades are always being produced, presenting the flower arranger with interesting new colour combinations and types.
CARE Cut the stem ends cleanly at a 45° angle with a sharp florist's knife, then condition the stems in a container of fresh water and flower food for several hours or overnight.

Scabiosa (scabious) p. 88
This attractive perennial flower is available in white and blue. Cut scabious from the garden or buy from the florist when the delicate flower head is half open.
CARE Place stems in deep water and flower food for a few hours.

Scilla (bluebell) p. 38
A spring flower found growing in woodlands, but it should not be picked from the wild. Both blue and white cultivated hybrids can be bought from florists in spring and will last up to a week in displays.
CARE Cut the stem ends at an angle and soak in fresh water and flower food for a few hours before arranging.

Senecio cineraria (senecio) p. 96
Attractive silver-grey foliage plant producing clusters of small vivid yellow flowers.
CARE Cut stem ends at an angle and place in lukewarm water for a few hours before arranging.

Stephanandra tanakae
(stephanandra vine) p. 78
This vine has arching branches of foliage and is available in autumn. The flexible branches are long-lasting and can be twisted around a wreath base to decorative effect.
CARE Cut stems at an angle and soak in clean water.

Symphoricarpos (snowberry) p. 96
Used mainly for their pink and white pearly berries, these are among the first autumn berry plants to appear.
CARE Remove excess leaves and cut stem ends at an angle before soaking in clean water.

Tropaeolum (nasturtium) p. 74
Long-lasting edible flowers with bright orange or red flowers which are used to decorate dining tables and salads.
CARE Cut the stem ends at an angle and place in clean water. Make sure that the flowers are free of black-fly before use.

Viburnum opulus (guelder rose)
pp. 38, 56, 88
Lobed deep-green leaves, with fragrant white flowers and clusters of red berries.
CARE Cut stem ends cleanly at an angle and place in clean water with flower food for several hours.

Viburnum tinus (viburnum) p. 92
A very useful plant in winter, when other foliage and flowers are scarce. It produces pink buds and then forms pretty, white star-shaped flowers between late autumn and early spring. The foliage is available throughout the year for use in displays.
CARE Cut stem ends cleanly at an angle and place in clean water with flower food for several hours.

suppliers

FRESH AND DRIED FLOWERS

Local florists and supermarkets are a good source of inexpensive fresh flowers, while large department stores often stock a good selection of dried flowers and seed heads.

Flowers & Plants Association
266–270 Flower Market
New Covent Garden Market
London SW8 5NB
www.flowers.org.uk
Organization that can be contacted for advice and tips on flower care.

Paula Pryke Flowers
Order line 020 7837 7336
paula@paula-pryke-flowers.com
www.paula-pryke-flowers.com

Paula Pryke Flowers @ Liberty
Great Marlborough Street
London W1R 6AH
020 7573 9563

Paula Pryke Flowers @ Brompton Cross
Michelin House
81 Fulham Road
London SW3 6RD
020 7589 4986

Martin Robinson Flowers
111 Walton Street
London SW3 2HP
Good selection of freeze-dried roses and other flowers.

Cameron Shaw Dried Flowers
279 New Kings Road
London SW6 4RD
Preserved and dried flowers.

FLORISTRY COURSES

Paula Pryke Flowers
The Flower House
3–5 Cynthia Street
London N1 9JF
tel: 020 7837 7373
fax: 020 7837 6766
www.paula-pryke-flowers.com
Contact for details of courses on flower arranging, as well as on wreaths, garlands and candle decorations, which demonstrate the ideas featured in this book.

FLORIST'S SUPPLIES & EQUIPMENT

Local garden centres are a wonderful source for most florist's equipment, including floral foam, tools, wreath bases, wires and string.

Avant Garden Centre
77 Ledbury Road
London W11 2AG
Good stock of pots, tools and string.

Chatsworth
31 Norwich Road
Strumpshaw
Norwich
Norfolk NR13 4AG
Fake fir wreaths, swags and Christmas decorations. Mail order.

The Chelsea Gardener
125 Sydney Street
London SW3 6NR
www.chelseagardener.com
All kinds of gardening equipment, floral foam and flowerpots.

Clifton Nurseries
5a Clifton Villas
London W9 2PH
www.clifton.co.uk
Loads of plants and flowerpots.

Diddybox
132–134 Belmont Road
Astley Bridge
Bolton BL1 7AN
Flower arrangers' sundries, including willow wreaths.

Pots and Pithoi
The Barns
East Street
Turners Hill
West Sussex RH10 4QQ
info@pots-and-pithoi.co.uk
Wonderful selection of old and new and handmade Cretan pots. Plus recycled Cretan glassware and painted china.

Simply Garlands
51 Albion Road
Pitstone
Bedfordshire
LU7 9AY
Fresh and dried garland bases. Mail order.

Smithers-Oasis UK Ltd
Crowther Road
Crowther Industrial Estate
Washington
Tyne & Wear NE38 0AQ
www.smithersoasis.com
Manufacturers of accessories for flower arranging and a complete range of floral foam products, including bricks and wreath frames, in a vast range of sizes and shapes.

Something Special
Station Road
Betchworth
Surrey RH3 7BZ
Floral and craft sundries.

Joanna Wood
48a Pimlico Road
London SW1W 8LP
www.joannawood.com
Decorative accessories, including cherubs and pine cones.

The Van Hage Garden Company
Great Armwell
Nr Ware
Hertfordshire SG12 9RP
www.vanhage.co.uk
Everything for the garden enthusiast.

DIY STORES

Larger stores sell a good selection of plants, tools and florist's sundries.

B&Q
Branches nationwide; for your nearest branch phone 0845 222 1000.
www.b&q.co.uk

Homebase
Branches nationwide; for your nearest branch phone 0870 900 8098.
www.homebase.co.uk

FABRICS, BUTTONS & RIBBONS

Department stores, haberdashery shops and local markets usually offer a good selection of colourful fabrics, unusual buttons and beautiful ribbons.

Borovick Fabrics Ltd
16 Berwick Street
London W1V 4HP
www.borovickfabricsltd.co.uk
Wide selection of silks and other fabrics.

Designers Guild
277 King's Road
London SW3 5EN
www.designersguild.com
Distinctive bright cottons in florals
and checks.

John Lewis Partnership Ltd
278–306 Oxford Street
London W1C 1EX
www.john-lewis-partnership.co.uk
Haberdashery, fabrics and great
scissors.

V V Rouleaux
54 Sloane Square
Cliveden Place
London SW1W 8AX
www.vvrouleaux.com
Wonderful selection of ribbons in
many widths and textures, including
wire-edged ribbon.

HERBS & SPICES
If your local supermarket or garden
centre cannot supply you with the
herbs or spices you require, try the
following specialists.

Culpeper Ltd
Unit 8 The Market
Covent Garden
London WC2E 8RB
www.culpeper.co.uk

Hexham Herbs
Chesters Walled Garden
Humshaugh
Hexham
Northumberland NE46 4BQ
www.chesterswalledgarden.
   fsnet.co.uk

Iden Croft Herbs
Frittenden Road
Staplehurst
Kent TN12 ODH
www.herbs-uk.com

The Spice Shop
1 Blenheim Crescent
London W11 2EE
www.thespiceshop.co.uk

PAINTS, PAPER & CRAFT EQUIPMENT
The following shops sell silver and gold
spray paint, coloured tissue paper and
other artist's materials you may need
to construct your wreaths.

Fred Aldous
PO Box 135
37 Lever Street
Manchester 1 M60 1UX
www.fredaldous.co.uk
Craft materials by mail order.

Paperchase
213 Tottenham Court Road
London W1T 7PS
www.paperchase.co.uk
Wonderful selection of paper, craft
materials and other decorative items.

Specialist Crafts Ltd
Unit 2
Wanlip Road Industrial Estate
Syston
Leicester LE7 1PA
www.speccrafts.co.uk
Craft supplies of all types. Mail order.

Stuart Stevenson
68 Clerkenwell Road
London
EC1M 5QA
Artist's materials.

STONES & SHELLS
Walks along the beach or in the
country often yield interesting finds:
driftwood, shells, pebbles and cones.

Civil Engineering Developments
Trout Road
West Drayton
Middx UB7 7RS
Unusual stones and pebbles.

Neal Street East
5–7 Neal Street
London
WC2H 9QL
All types of shells, paper flowers,
plus raffia, caning, and lots of other
materials from around the world.
Mail order.

ACCESSORIES
Visit the following stores for stylish
accessories, such as china, metal and
glass dishes, vases and containers, as
well as candles and candle holders.

Celestial Buttons
162 Archway Road
Highgate
London N6 5BB
020 8341 2788
Wide range of accessories, feathers,
ribbons and buttons.

The Conran Shop
Michelin House
81 Fulham Road
London SW3 6RD
www.conranshop.co.uk

Habitat
Branches nationwide; for your nearest
branch phone 0845 601 0740.
www.habitat.net

Heal's
196 Tottenham Court Road
London W1T 9LG
www.heals.co.uk

IKEA
Branches nationwide; for your nearest
branch phone 020 8208 5600.
www.ikea.co.uk

Liberty plc
214–20 Regent Street
London W1B 5AH
www.liberty.co.uk

Marston & Langinger Ltd
192 Mozart Terrace
Ebury Street
London SW1W 8UP
www.marston-and-langinger.com

The Pier
200 Tottenham Court Road
London W1T 7PL
www.pier.co.uk

Selfridges
400 Oxford Street
London W1A 1AB
020 7629 1234 and branches
www.selfridges.co.uk

Skandium
86–87 Marylebone High Street
London W1U 4QT
020 7935 2077
www.skandium.com
(Also concessions at Selfridges in
Birmingham, London and
Manchester)

acknowledgements

It has been my great pleasure to work on this book with such an accomplished photographer as James Merrell. James and I have been shooting three books simultaneously to capture all the seasons for each one, and I am extremely grateful to him for bringing his unique blend of good humour, calm intuition and artistic talent to each day. His patience and endurance are inspirational!

I am also grateful to the extremely artistic and imaginative stylists who have worked on this book, Nato Welton, Martin Bourne and Margaret Caselton, who have brought their own personal style and expertise to this project. I must also thank the talented illustrator, Helen Smythe, for her superb artworks.

Thank you to the long-suffering staff at Ryland Peters & Small for all their support in the making of this volume, especially Paul Tilby and Zia Mattocks.

I am also grateful to the extremely resourceful and accomplished duo, Colin Walton and Bella Pringle, who were so charming and professional to work with.

As always, I am extremely grateful to all my own staff who contributed time and ideas to this book, and also to those who carried on the day-to-day business while I was away. Thanks especially to Ashleigh Hopkins, who continues to support me and manage the business – not to mention her input to the company as a gifted and accomplished florist. In recent years my school has become very popular in Japan and I am extremely happy to have had the assistance on this project of Shinako Atsumi, Mikiko Tanabe, Hiroko Odakura, Fumiko Inoue, Yoko Okasaki and Tomoko Akamine. They have all studied with me during the course and have, in their own way, contributed many ideas and suggestions, and have painstakingly created some of the intricate designs.

I am also very grateful to Joan Cardoza for all her help with this book and for her calm and resourceful manner and artistic input. Anita Everard was also called in to help me keep up with James Merrell's speedy photography, and to contribute her immense talent and experience. Thank you also to my personal assistants, Jane Houghton and Sophie Hindley.

A very special thank you to all my colleagues and friends at New Covent Garden Flower Market, especially Dennis Edwards and all at John Austin & Co. Ltd. Thanks also to Toby at Celestial Buttons, C Best, Something Special, Gerhard Jenne at Konditor & Cook, Jim Brazier, The Peasant Restaurant, Chris Johnson at Sia Parlane and Peter Lethbridge for their help with this project. Finally, a very personal thank you to Terence Conran for encouraging me to make bigger and better wreaths each Christmas!

credits

Page 10 Bottom right striped fabric: Designers Guild.
Page 68 Bottom right butterfly fabric: Osborne & Little; fabric butterflies: V V Rouleaux.
Page 91 Marble plates and bowls: David Wainwright.